You're Already Her

You're Already Her

Stop Waiting, Start Living in Your Magic

Alicia Arlene

JOSSEY-BASS™
A Wiley Brand

Published by John Wiley & Sons, Inc., Hoboken, New Jersey.

Library of Congress Cataloging-in-Publication Data:

Names: Arlene, Alicia author
Title: You're already her : stop waiting, start living in your magic / Alicia Arlene.
Other titles: You are already her
Description: Hoboken, New Jersey : Wiley, [2027] | Includes index.
Identifiers: LCCN 2026021523 (print) | LCCN 2026021524 (ebook) | ISBN 9781394374427 cloth | ISBN 9781394374441 adobe pdf | ISBN 9781394374434 epub
Subjects: LCSH: Self-actualization (Psychology) in women
Classification: LCC BF637.S4 A7345 2027 (print) | LCC BF637.S4 (ebook)
LC record available at https://lccn.loc.gov/2026021523
LC ebook record available at https://lccn.loc.gov/2026021524

Cover Design: Wiley
Cover Image: detshana/stock.adobe.com
Author Photo: Courtesy of the Author
Printed and bound by CPI Group (UK) Ltd, Croydon, CR0 4YY

C9781394374427_080826

For my daughter, Madilynn Laureen. My guardian angel sent me you, the brightest reminder that becoming the woman I'm meant to be matters. You are my favorite person to laugh with, my safest place to land, and the one who makes everything feel lighter. You are my heart in human form. You've made me stronger, softer, and braver in every way. I hope one day you read these words and feel proud to call me your mom and know that so much of this book was written with you in my heart. Always.

Contents

Introduction

I didn't write this book because I had everything figured out. I wrote it because for years, I didn't. I wrote it because I know what it feels like to wake up and wonder if you're ever going to feel like the woman you always pictured in your head. I know what it feels like to carry stories that were never yours, to shrink in rooms where something in you forgot you belonged, to look at your life and quietly think, *There has to be more than this.* And if you've ever felt that way—even for a moment—then this book is for you.

I wrote this book because no woman should have to guess her way into her own life. I don't want you to go through life pretending you're fine, shrinking yourself to survive rooms you were never meant to fit into. I don't want you waking up years from now realizing you built a life that kept everyone else comfortable while you quietly disappeared inside it.

You deserve better than that. You deserve to know yourself. You deserve to live in your magic. You deserve to live a life that feels so damn good inside.

This book isn't here to fix you. You were never broken. It's here to walk with you. To remind you of who you are when the noise gets loud. To give you language for the things you've felt but never named. To help you stop waiting for confidence to appear and start living as the woman who's been trying to get your attention for years.

And as you move through these pages, read them like a woman who's done negotiating with her own potential. Let them shift you, soften you, and show you the strength you've been carrying this whole time. You're stepping into a new chapter of your life, and this time, you're leading the way.

Part One

THE TRUTH THAT SETS YOU FREE

Part One is where everything finally starts to make sense. You don't instantly become the woman you want to be, but for the first time, you can clearly see why you haven't felt like her yet. This isn't the part where you transform. This is the part where the fog lifts. The struggle isn't a lack of desire or ambition. It's the quiet sense that something in your life feels slightly off. Not broken or disastrous. Just quietly misaligned in a way that's hard to put into words. Maybe that's where you are right now. You love parts of your life. You're grateful for what you have. But there's a part of you—a small, steady hum—that keeps whispering, *I thought I'd feel different than this.* Not necessarily unhappy. Just not fully you.

Part One is where we look back so you can understand the identity you've been carrying without realizing it—the one that taught you to be agreeable instead of honest, selfless instead of self-connected, strong instead of supported. The version of you who learned to shrink because shrinking felt safer. You didn't choose these patterns. You inherited them. You adapted to them. You survived with them. And now, you're starting to outgrow them.

This section of the book will help you finally put words to the things you've felt for years: the exhaustion that isn't fixed by sleep, the low-grade ache of wanting more, the quiet sense that you've become the dependable one while losing parts of yourself along the way. It's not heavy—it's honest. And it's the honesty that sets you free.

Part One isn't about becoming her. It's about understanding why you haven't let yourself be her yet. By the time you turn the page into Part Two, you won't just feel seen—you'll feel yourself waking back up. Not in some big, obvious way. Not all at once. But enough to whisper, *Okay . . . I'm ready now.*

Chapter 1

The Moment You Start Coming Home to Yourself

You don't forget the moments that split your life in two. Something inside you rearranges so completely that you can never go back to who you were before. For me, that moment wasn't a glow-up. It wasn't a revelation wrapped in clarity. It was 3 a.m. in a dim, stale camp room at a gold mine in the Yukon—the kind of room with buzzing lights, thin walls, and a heaviness that sinks into your skin. I was 25, exhausted, and barely holding on. And somewhere inside my chest, the girl I'd spent a decade abandoning finally asked, *Are you done yet?*

The Beginning of Everything

People look at the woman I am now and assume I felt sure of myself when I left. I didn't. There was no clarity, no confidence, just this quiet, aching realization that if I didn't move, if I didn't do something right then, I was going to disappear into a version of myself I wouldn't recognize. Or disappear completely.

But to understand why that moment mattered, you need to understand who I was long before that night. You need to understand the girl who walked into that camp room already cracked in ways no one could see.

When I was 15, my mom died from cancer. Even though it didn't happen "suddenly," it felt sudden and brutal, without giving me a chance to breathe before the ground disappeared beneath me. She wasn't just my mom. She was the place I went to feel understood. The proof that I was worthy just by existing. I didn't just lose my mother. I lost the one person in this whole entire world who made me feel like I didn't have to prove anything to be loved. I didn't have to perform. I didn't have to play nice to be accepted. I was loved for just being Alicia. For existing.

When she passed away, the world didn't just get darker. It got louder. Expectations. Opinions. Assumptions about who I should be and how I should cope. And without her, I learned a new belief that at the time I didn't have words for yet: love wasn't something you received. It was something you earned. Worthiness wasn't inherent. It was conditional. My value depended on how little space I took up, how easy I was to manage, and how much I could swallow without making anyone else uncomfortable.

That's the identity I carried into my teens and 20s. Not the identity of a girl who didn't care. The identity of a girl who cared so deeply she believed the only way to be loved was to become smaller than her own needs. I became the girl who apologized before she spoke. The girl who laughed at things that hurt. The girl who dated people who didn't choose her fully because she didn't believe she deserved to be chosen. The girl who over-performed, over-accommodated, and over-functioned until she had nothing left.

By the time I met the man I would eventually leave in that Yukon camp, my self-worth wasn't broken—it was borrowed. Borrowed from other people's emotions. Borrowed from their approval. Borrowed from whether or not they thought I was lovable. I didn't have a stable sense of myself, so I clung to anyone who made me feel like I wasn't completely unfixable.

And that's how you end up in situations you never imagined yourself tolerating. It isn't weakness or being naive. It's the slow erosion of your own inner voice. The kind that happens so gradually you barely notice it. Until one day you realize you're no longer choosing from love, but reacting from survival.

That relationship wasn't all bad—that's what makes it so hard to walk away. It was the good moments that convinced me the bad ones weren't that bad. The apologies. The promises. The brief stretches of calm that made me believe we were turning a corner. But underneath it all were patterns I had learned to live inside without question. I didn't even know who I was back then, so the idea that I deserved something different never even crossed my mind.

I became a version of myself that could withstand anything, tolerate anything, justify anything, as long as it didn't require me to choose myself.

And then came that night.

The message on my phone wasn't new. The manipulation wasn't new. The knot in my stomach wasn't new. What *was* new was the silence that came after reading it—not the silence in the room, but the silence inside me. The part of me that usually defended him. The part of me that usually explained it away. The part of me that usually begged for crumbs. For the first time in years, those parts didn't speak. Instead, something deeper broke through. Something older. Something that sounded a lot like the girl I was before life got heavy.

Get up.

It didn't feel big in the moment. It wasn't empowering. It was a truth so simple it felt ancient. Get up. Move. Leave. And for reasons I still can't fully explain, I listened. I grabbed my bag. I shoved clothes into it with shaking hands. I threw my life into the back seat of my car and started driving south, toward Saskatchewan, toward home, toward something I didn't have a name for yet.

That drive was the longest and shortest of my life. The sun rose as my world fell apart. I cried until I couldn't breathe. I talked myself in and out of turning around at least 50 times. I tried to convince myself I was overreacting, that it wasn't that bad, that maybe if I just tried harder, I could hold it all together. And every time my phone buzzed—the apologies, the "I love you," the pleas, the guilt—the old identity in me stirred.

The truth women rarely say out loud is when you leave someone who hurts you, the part that still loves them doesn't die instantly. And the part of you that believes you don't deserve better fights like hell to pull you back.

But that morning, the pull of survival was louder. And survival isn't pretty. It's not empowered. It's not confident. It's raw. It's primal. It's the part of you that grabs your own hand and says, *If we don't go now, we may never go.* That's what carried me home.

But the moment that truly changed everything came hours later. I stopped at a Walmart because my whole body felt empty. I walked the aisles in a haze, unsure what I was even looking for. And then I saw it—a pink journal. Cheap, blank, nothing special. I don't know why I picked it up. I don't know why I held it to my chest like it was something sacred. But I did.

I sat in my car in that parking lot and opened it. I wrote like my life depended on it—because in a way, it did. I wrote about the woman I wanted to become. I wrote about the life I didn't believe I deserved but hoped I could grow into. I wrote about wanting softness, stability, joy, self-respect. And even though I didn't feel like her at all, even though my hands were trembling and my face was blotchy from crying, something inside me whispered, *This is the first time you chose you.*

I didn't become a different woman that night. I didn't suddenly believe in myself. I didn't walk into some confident era. I simply stopped abandoning myself long enough to hear the truth that had been buried under a decade of survival:

> *You don't need to earn the right to love yourself. You simply need to stop leaving yourself.*

That's where this book really begins. Not with confidence or empowerment. But with the moment you stop negotiating your worth and start choosing yourself in real time—even when it's messy, even when you're terrified, and even when you don't believe you deserve it yet.

Because confidence didn't carry me out of the Yukon. Identity did. The identity of a woman who was finally done disappearing. The identity of a woman who didn't want to keep living a life she had to convince herself she was grateful for. The identity of a woman who chose movement over permission.

And that's what I want you to understand before you go any further:

> *Your life doesn't change when you feel ready. It changes when you stop abandoning yourself.*

Not always in the grand, cinematic moments, but in the quiet ones when you decide you deserve more than the identity you outgrew.

This is where your shift begins, too. Not with perfectionism or confidence or a flawless plan, but with honesty. With awareness. With past self-reflection. With the courage to hear your own voice again. The one that's been whispering under all the noise:

> *Get up. Move. Choose yourself.*

This Is Where It Shows Up in Your Life

That moment in the Yukon wasn't when I abandoned myself. It was the moment I finally stopped. The kind that forces you to stop and look at your life differently. The kind you can't ignore.

But most of the time, it doesn't look like that.

Most of the time, it's quiet. It shows up in the smallest, most normal parts of your day. In the way you second-guess what you were about to say, in the way you talk yourself out of something you want, in the way you adjust, accommodate, or shrink without even realizing you're doing it.

It doesn't feel like self-abandonment when it's happening. But it adds up.

Over time, those small moments shape how you see yourself. What you believe you're allowed to want. How much space you think you're allowed to take up. What kind of life you think is available to you. That's how you end up waiting.

Waiting to feel more confident. Waiting to feel more ready. Waiting to feel like the kind of woman who would choose differently. Not realizing the waiting is the pattern. Not realizing those small moments are the reason nothing changes.

And once you start seeing that, you can't unsee it.

The Micro-Moments That Show You Who You Really Are

Let's talk about a universal moment in every woman's life: the girls' night group chat. The "what's everyone wearing?" messages. The rapid-fire replies. The quiet panic that makes you second-guess the outfit you were excited about five minutes ago. For me, that moment didn't happen during a confident era or a carefree season. It happened the summer I left the Yukon—the summer I was trying to rebuild a life that didn't feel like it belonged to me yet. I was back home living at my dad's, still fragile, still unsure, still trying to figure out who I was now that the life I had pictured for myself had completely collapsed. Most days, I felt like I was holding myself together with hope and duct tape. But underneath the heaviness, there was this tiny flicker of something—desire, maybe. A quiet craving to feel alive again. So, when my friends texted me about going out, I felt a little spark. I wanted to feel pretty. I wanted to feel chosen—by myself, not by a man, not by a circumstance, not by someone's version of who I should be. I wanted to feel even a glimpse of the woman I hoped I could become.

I went to my closet, which at that point was just a cheap metal rack holding the pieces of my life I hadn't given up on yet. And hanging there was the red dress. Not a fancy dress, not expensive, not something anyone else would think twice about—but to me, it felt like possibility. It was bold, bright, a little risky. It felt like the kind of dress you buy when you're trying to convince yourself you still have a future worth dressing up for. I held it against my body and for a split second, I could see her—the woman who wore color unapologetically, who didn't shrink, who didn't apologize for attention, who didn't wait for permission to shine. It was a moment of remembering, even though I didn't know that's what it was at the time.

Then my phone buzzed. The girls sent their outfits: jeans and a cute top. Jeans and a sweater. Jeans and a bodysuit because "it's kind of chilly out." All perfectly reasonable outfits for a casual night out. Safe. Predictable. Expected. And I remember staring at my red dress—this tiny symbol of the woman I wanted to be—and immediately talking myself out of it. I didn't want to be overdressed. I didn't want to be the dramatic one. I didn't want anyone thinking I was trying too hard. I didn't want attention, not when I still felt like a version of myself I barely recognized. I didn't want to look like I was becoming someone new before I had earned it.

So I hung up the dress and put it back. I reached for my jeans. And I told myself it didn't matter. *But it did matter.* It was the instant reflex. The automatic shrinking. The way I abandoned the smallest spark of myself just to blend in. Looking back now, that night was one of the first breadcrumbs that led me into my identity work. It was subtle, easy to miss, but it was truth. The truth that I was living from habit, not intention. Fear, not desire. Familiarity, not identity.

We always picture identity shifts as big, obvious moments—the 3 a.m. breaking point, the cross-country move, the relationship ending, the new beginning. But most shifts? They start in moments like this. In the small choices where you feel a pull toward something braver, bolder, more aligned—and you talk yourself out of it without even thinking. The red dress is just a metaphor, but every woman has her version of it. The thing she wants but doesn't choose. The expression she suppresses. The truth she edits. The desire she dims. Not to protect herself, but to protect the comfort of the room around her. We don't shrink because we're weak. We shrink because we've been conditioned to. We've been taught that being "too much" is dangerous, that wanting more is ungrateful, that shining without permission is arrogant. So we tone ourselves down, one micro-moment at a time.

What I didn't see then—but so clearly see now—is that identity isn't built in the breakthroughs. It's built in these tiny, forgettable moments where you either choose truth or choose safety. And I had been choosing safety for so long, it felt natural. It felt responsible. It felt like the only option. But that night, something in me ached. I didn't know why. I didn't know what it meant. I just knew that I had seen a glimpse of the woman I wanted to be, and I had put her back on a hanger. The ache wasn't about the dress. It was about the abandonment. It was about the quiet realization that the thing keeping me small wasn't my past, or my circumstances, or my fear—*it was me*. I was the one deciding not to choose myself. And that realization, even in the smallest dose, stays with you.

Once you see yourself putting the red dress back, you can't unsee it. You start recognizing the pattern, not just the moment. You realize it's not about one decision, it's about how often you've been choosing what feels acceptable over what feels true. And that awareness changes how you move, because now you know it's happening in real time.

That summer, I was rebuilding my life, but I didn't yet understand that rebuilding happens from the inside out. Not through grand gestures, but through micro-moments when you choose something different. That night was one of the first. It didn't feel like transformation. It didn't feel like a lesson. It felt like jeans, a bar, laughing with my friends while wishing I had chosen the dress. But that's how identity shifts start—quietly, humbly, through tiny decisions that don't match who you want to be.

And here's the secret no one tells you: your identity is shaped long before your life catches up. You become her in moments where nothing looks like her yet. You become her by choosing something small and honest, even when it scares you. You become her by noticing when you shrink—and deciding not to next time. That night didn't transform me. But it woke me up. It showed me that alignment isn't a big leap. It's a hundred tiny adjustments. And every adjustment matters, because every adjustment is a vote for who you're becoming.

If I had worn the red dress, my life wouldn't have magically changed. But something in me would have shifted sooner. My relationship with myself would have softened sooner. My self-trust would have grown sooner. Because that's what these decisions really are: micro-moments of self-loyalty. Micro-moments of coming back home. Micro-moments that whisper, *I see you. I choose you.* And those moments compound. They build strength. They build identity. They build a woman who doesn't abandon herself—not even on the small things.

Looking back, that summer was full of missed red-dress moments—times when I didn't choose myself, times when I ignored desire, times when I played small out of habit. But every time I felt that familiar ache, it was a reminder: you're meant for more than the safe version of you. You're meant for the truth of you. Not someday. Not when everything feels stable. Now.

And that's what this chapter is about. Not a deep dive into self-worth—that comes later. This chapter is about *awareness.* About seeing the tiny decisions that shape your identity long before you even realize you're making them. It's about understanding that becoming the woman you want to be doesn't start with the big, brave moment. It starts the night you wish you wore the red dress. It starts with noticing when you abandon yourself—and why. It starts with the tiny sparks that already exist inside you, even when your life still feels like pieces scattered on the floor.

Rebuilding starts long before the world sees it. It starts in the quiet, private, seemingly insignificant moments when you decide who you're going to be, even if you're not ready to become her yet.

And the beauty? You don't need to get it perfect. You just need to start noticing. So the next time you feel that spark, that pull, that whisper of *this feels like me . . .*

I hope you listen.
I hope you trust it.
I hope you wear the damn dress.

Why Confidence Isn't What You Think It Is

For most of your life, you've been taught that confidence is a feeling. Something you're supposed to wake up with. Something that magically appears once you finally "get your life together," hit a milestone, fix a flaw, or reinvent yourself into someone easier to admire. No one ever said those words out loud, but you learned the lesson anyway. You learned it in classrooms where speaking up felt dangerous, in friendships where you weren't sure your voice mattered, in family systems that praised achievement more than authenticity, in relationships where shrinking felt safer than being fully seen. Confidence became something you thought you had to earn, and because you didn't feel it, you assumed you hadn't earned enough yet.

But that's not how confidence works at all. Confidence isn't a feeling you wait for. It isn't a personality trait you either lucked into or missed out on. It isn't some inner electricity that only turns on once you've healed enough, glowed up enough, or become "the best version" of yourself. Confidence is simpler than you've been taught. Confidence is identity behavior. It's the way you show up long before your emotions catch up. It's the decision to back yourself even when your stomach is in a knot and your hands won't stop sweating. It's the moment you trust your internal yes enough to follow it, even when your old self is whispering all the reasons you shouldn't.

When you strip it all back, confidence has nothing to do with feeling ready. It has everything to do with choosing to act like a woman you haven't fully met yet—and letting the feeling come later.

That's why so many women think they "struggle with confidence," when the truth is they've just been taught to wait for it. To wait until the fear calms down, until the nerves settle, until the self-doubt disappears. To wait until life feels perfectly lined up so they can finally show up fully. But readiness is a feeling—and feelings are terrible leaders. Confidence isn't what happens when your nerves go quiet. Confidence is what happens when you stop letting your nerves be the reason you don't move.

Think back to my red-dress moment—not the dress itself, but the part I didn't even recognize at the time. Confidence wasn't missing from that night. Confidence was just misunderstood. I was waiting to *feel* bold enough to wear the thing I wanted. But confidence was hiding in the discomfort. It was in the part of me that wanted the dress in the first place. It was in the flicker of truth I didn't think I was allowed to follow yet. The jeans didn't win because they felt better. The jeans won because they felt safer. And that's the trap so many women live inside: mistaking safety for truth, mistaking comfort for alignment, mistaking invisibility for peace.

Most of us don't struggle with confidence; we struggle with permission. Permission to take up space. Permission to want what we want without apologizing. Permission to be seen without rehearsing the perfect version of ourselves first. Permission to live a life that feels like ours, even if it means stepping into rooms we're not sure we belong in yet. And because we never learned how to give ourselves that permission, we keep waiting for the world to hand it to us. We keep waiting for the feeling of confidence to show up first so we can finally make the move.

Confidence doesn't come first. The decision does. And in the beginning, that decision won't feel empowering, it will feel uncomfortable. You'll question it almost immediately. You'll want to soften it, take it back, make it easier for everyone else to receive. But if you don't, if you let the moment stand, you start to notice something shift. You trust yourself faster. You spend less time going back and forth in your head. What used to feel like a big deal starts to feel normal. And at some point, without even realizing when it happened, you're just moving differently. That's confidence. Not something you wait for, but something that catches up to you after you've already started.

This is why so many women don't recognize their own strength—because they expect it to feel magical. They expect confidence to feel like instant clarity, steady hands, and a calm chest. But confidence often feels like a trembling voice that speaks anyway. It feels like a shaky breath before you send the message you've been avoiding. It feels like wearing the dress your fear told you not to wear. It feels like walking into the room where the old version of you would've stayed home. Confidence isn't the absence of nerves. It's the presence of self-leadership.

When this clicks, things start to change. Confidence stops being something you chase and becomes something you practice. It becomes a daily identity choice: Am I going to reinforce the story that keeps me small, or am I going to step into the story I want to live? Am I going to move like the woman who trusts herself or like the one who still negotiates her worth with every decision? Am I going to let comfort lead or let truth lead? Suddenly the question isn't, *How do I feel more confident?* The real question is, *What would I do right now if I trusted myself?*

When you ask yourself that, the answers come quickly: You'd wear the outfit you keep saving for the more confident version of you. You'd say the thing you've been rehearsing in your head. You'd raise your rates, raise your standards, and stop accepting the bare minimum from people who never have to deal with the consequences of your self-abandonment. You'd pick the life you want instead of the one that offends the fewest people. You'd lead your decisions instead of letting fear lead your imagination.

Confidence is identity. That's what no one tells you. It's who you decide to be in the moments that matter—not who you already feel like. The woman you're becoming doesn't wait for permission. She doesn't negotiate her truth with her fear. She doesn't outsource her decisions to the group chat, the algorithm, or the version of herself who learned to stay small to stay safe.

She leads. She moves. She chooses. And every time she does, she becomes easier for you to access.

This is why confidence isn't what you think it is. It's not a feeling. It's a pattern. It's a relationship with yourself. It's the accumulation of tiny, inconvenient, uncurated acts of self-loyalty—the ones no one sees but you. And once you understand that, you stop waiting. You stop negotiating. You stop postponing your life until some imaginary version of you appears to take over. You realize the confident woman you've been imagining isn't a future version you need to earn—she's a current version you need to practice.

You don't need to become someone else to feel confident. You need to stop abandoning the woman you already are.

The Choice Shift Framework

At some point, a realization begins to take shape, one that changes how you see yourself entirely. You're not stuck because you're weak, unmotivated, or missing some magical confidence gene. You're stuck because you've been living your life from the same choice you've made years ago—a choice you didn't even know you were making. A choice to stay small, stay agreeable, stay quiet, stay easy. A choice to protect yourself instead of expressing yourself. A choice to survive instead of self-lead. And because you've made that same choice hundreds of times without realizing it, it's become a loop: familiar, predictable, safe . . . and suffocating.

This isn't the kind of loop you see. It's the kind you feel. The one where you know exactly what you want to say, but the words stay trapped behind your teeth. The one where you feel the spark to do something bold, but the fear of being "too much" smothers it. The one where you get dressed, love your outfit, then change last minute because you imagine the way someone might look at you. The one where you've never missed a deadline at work, but your own dreams have been sitting on the back burner for years. The one where you feel alive in flashes—then immediately retreat back into the version of yourself that feels safer to operate from.

This is the *old choice*—the unconscious decision to shrink. To prioritize comfort over truth. To prioritize acceptance over authenticity. To prioritize other people's reactions over your own alignment.

Most of us don't even realize we're making this choice. We just feel the heaviness of it. The frustration. The stuckness. The quiet, aching awareness that we're living a life that's technically fine, but not fully ours. It's not that we don't want more. It's that the old choice has been rehearsed for so long, our nervous system has mistaken it for identity.

But here's what actually matters: confidence doesn't interrupt the loop. Awareness doesn't interrupt the loop. Wanting more for yourself doesn't interrupt the loop. Those things help, but they don't create change.

Only a *new choice* does.

That new choice begins in a moment that doesn't look important at all. One small, inconvenient decision when you would usually abandon yourself. Saying the honest thing instead of the easy thing. Letting your yes be yes, and your no be no. The moment you choose the outfit you love instead of the one that hides you. The moment you stop rehearsing the reaction and start trusting your intention. The moment you choose peace over performance, truth over optics, alignment over approval.

That new choice is what I call *the shift*—the micro-moment when you catch the old pattern rising in your chest, and you interrupt it by choosing something that honors the woman you want to be, not the one you've outgrown.

You may not feel powerful when it happens. You may feel shaky and unsure. Your heart might race. Your throat might tighten. Your fear might try to negotiate with you. But the shift doesn't require you to feel ready—it only requires you to choose differently.

And here's the wild part: the moment you do, your brain updates the story it's been telling about you. It starts to gather new evidence. It rewrites who you believe you are based on how you just acted. That one choice becomes proof. Proof that you can trust yourself. Proof that you won't abandon yourself. Proof that you're done rehearsing the smaller version of you.

Do that once, and it feels unfamiliar. Do it twice, and something inside you starts to perk up. Do it 10 times, and you start to notice that your default settings don't feel like default anymore. They feel like options—not obligations.

That's how identity shifts: through repeated, intentional choices that contradict the old narrative. Through everyday moments where you decide, I'm not going back to who I was.

The more you choose the shift, the more the old loop dissolves. You stop bracing for worst-case scenarios. You stop writing stories about what people might think. You stop editing yourself into the version you believe will be easiest to love. You stop turning your desires into inconveniences. You stop carrying guilt for being fully alive.

The shift does something even deeper, too—it recalibrates your energy. The world responds differently to you because *you* show up differently in it. Not louder, not flashier, not suddenly fearless . . . just truer. Clearer. More rooted in your own skin. People sense it. Opportunities find you. Conversations change. Boundaries hold. You stop chasing worthiness and start living from it. Not through outside validation or someone finally telling you you're enough. Through the quiet accumulation of choices that keep reinforcing what your mind hasn't fully believed yet: *you're already her.*

This is the biggest mistake people make about confidence—they treat it like a feeling. But confidence is built through the shift. Through evidence. Through repetition. Through choosing your future identity more often than you choose your past one.

So the real question isn't whether you're confident. The real question is, which choice are you rehearsing? The one that keeps you comfortable, or the one that builds the life you keep dreaming about?

Because every moment is an invitation. To repeat the old self, or to practice the new one. To stay in the loop, or to choose the shift. To keep waiting for your life to change, or to realize it already began the second you stopped abandoning yourself.

Confidence didn't change my life. Choices did. And the same will be true for you.

Shift 1: The Moment You Stop Hiding from Yourself

The first shift is easy to miss. It happens in a quiet moment when you finally stop arguing with yourself and tell the truth about what you want.

The real reason your confidence has felt shaky for so long is that you've been performing a version of yourself you don't identify with anymore. You've been staying loyal to an identity that doesn't fit, pretending it still feels safe when it actually feels suffocating. You've been rehearsing an old self out of habit, not desire.

Shift 1 is the moment you decide you're done with that. It's the moment you stop abandoning yourself in small ways and start catching the places where you shrink without even realizing it.

It happens in the places no one else pays attention to—the way you answer a question in a crowded room, the way you dodge a mirror, the way you laugh off a compliment, the way you soften your voice so no one thinks you're "too much." It's in the tiny pause between what you want to say and what you actually say. And it's in every moment you tell yourself, *It's not a big deal*, even though your body knows it is.

For most women, this shift starts where there's no audience to perform for. When you're alone with yourself and there's nowhere to hide from the truth. That's when the gap between who you are and who you've been pretending to be becomes impossible to ignore. That's when a new kind of honesty becomes possible.

> *The first shift is simply this: you stop lying to yourself about what you want, what you feel, and who you know you're meant to be.*

Confidence isn't built on being fearless. It's built on being truthful. You can't trust a woman who lies to herself about what she wants. And you can't build confidence inside an identity that isn't honest.

So instead of trying to "feel confident," this shift asks you to notice your own patterns with a gentleness you probably haven't given yourself in years. Notice how often you hold your tongue so you don't make things awkward. How often you edit your personality to match the room. How often you say yes while your stomach sinks. How often your reflection surprises you because it doesn't match the version of yourself you've been imagining in your mind.

You don't have to fix any of it yet. You don't have to rewrite the story overnight. This shift isn't about action. It's about awareness. It's about looking at yourself honestly without spiraling into judgment or shame. It's about finally seeing all the subtle places where you've been leaving yourself behind.

Because the smallest self-abandonments become the loudest identity wounds. And the smallest self-honesties become the strongest roots of self-trust.

Shift 1 is the moment you start catching yourself in real time. The moment you say, *Oh. There I go again. That's the version of me I'm outgrowing.* It's gentle. It's human. And it's powerful enough to change everything.

When you make this shift, your inner world rearranges itself. Decisions get clearer. Boundaries stop feeling like battles. Your desires stop feeling embarrassing and start feeling inevitable. You stop performing and start participating. You stop shrinking and start choosing. And for the first time in a long time, your internal world feels like somewhere you want to live.

Confidence doesn't start with a roar. It starts with a whisper: *this isn't who I am anymore.*

That's Shift 1. And once you make it, nothing in your life feels the same again.

Shift 2: Trusting Yourself Before You Feel Ready

You start noticing how often you're waiting for a green light that never actually comes. Waiting for permission to take the risk. To want more. To stop playing the version of yourself everyone else is comfortable with. To follow the pull in your chest even when it doesn't make sense yet. Something cracks open. Something says, *I can't keep waiting for proof I'm ready.*

Shift 2 is the moment you stop waiting.

This is the shift where you begin trusting yourself before you feel qualified, prepared, or perfectly healed. Where you stop needing a guarantee and start choosing yourself with nothing but a hunch and a heartbeat. We've been taught to earn our boldness: to wait for confidence like it's a diploma we get handed after we've performed well enough. But confidence isn't the pre-req. It's the by-product. You don't wait to feel ready. You move, and readiness builds around you.

This shift asks you to stop outsourcing "Can I handle this?" to other people's reactions, opinions, or instructions. To stop waiting for someone to tap you on the shoulder and say, "Okay, now go." It asks you to lead with desire instead of doubt, and to trust that the version of you who wants more isn't irresponsible—she's intuitive. She sees something your current circumstances haven't caught up to yet.

Trusting yourself before you feel ready is uncomfortable. It feels like stepping into a room before the lights turn on. Your body searches for something familiar. Your mind reaches for evidence you don't have yet. Your nervous system reminds you of every time you played big and got burned. And still, something in you whispers, *Go anyway.*

That whisper matters. It's your future self pulling you forward.

Most women never make this shift because they've been conditioned to believe they need certainty before they move. But certainty isn't a starting point. It's a privilege you earn by walking through the unknown and realizing you didn't fall apart.

You build trust with yourself the same way you do with anyone else—by showing up consistently, especially when it's inconvenient or intimidating.

This shift is where you stop asking, *What if I fail?* and start asking, *What if this is the moment everything changes?* Failure isn't what destroys you. Abandoning yourself is. And you already know what that feels like. You already know the cost of shrinking your life to fit an identity you've outgrown.

Trusting yourself before you're ready looks like sending the message, applying for the job, taking the class, booking the trip, starting the business, saying the truth, raising your hand, wearing the red dress, walking into the room—and refusing to let the old version of you narrate what you're capable of. It's moving because the desire is there, not because the fear is gone.

It also shows up quietly. It's how you stop double-checking your decisions with people who don't live with the consequences. How you stop tying your worth to how "reasonable" you appear. How you stop needing your feelings to be validated to be real. How you keep reminding yourself that you're allowed to choose what you know is right for you, even when you can't fully explain it yet.

Your intuition is data. Your desire is data. Your discomfort, frustration, and dreams are data. Trusting yourself isn't delusional—it's leadership. It's the moment you stop treating your inner knowing as a suggestion and start treating it like direction.

When you begin doing that—even in small, shaky, imperfect ways—your entire identity expands. You stop playing the supporting role in your own life. You stop waiting for perfect conditions. You stop abandoning the part of you that wants more. You step into a new gravitational pull where belief leads and confidence follows.

Trusting yourself before you're ready isn't about being reckless. It's about accepting that the woman you're becoming can't be built inside the lines the old you drew for safety. It's about letting your next chapter be bigger than your last wound.

Shift 2 is where things finally start to move. Not on the outside yet, but inside you. It's the moment you stop debating the voice that already knows where you're meant to go.

This is the shift where your identity stops being inherited and starts being chosen. And you're the one choosing it—even if your voice shakes, even if your hands tremble, even if you have no idea what the outcome will be. That's what makes it powerful. That's what makes it yours.

Shift 3: Stop Shaping Yourself for Rooms You've Outgrown

You realize you've been shrinking to fit spaces that were never designed for your expansion, spaces that only welcomed you as quiet, predictable, and agreeable. Spaces that praised you for being "easy" while draining every ounce of your aliveness. Spaces that rewarded you for who you used to be—not who you're becoming.

Shift 3 is the moment you stop doing that.

This is the shift where you stop molding yourself to meet the comfort levels of people who have no idea who you're trying to be. Where you stop shrinking your edges to keep the peace. Where you stop carrying identities you've outgrown simply because people learned to expect them from you. Many of the rooms you're still performing in are spaces you quietly stopped wanting a long time ago. Familiarity keeps you there, because being fully seen still feels like the bigger risk. This shift asks you to call out the quiet ways you've been shaping yourself for other people's benefit. The jokes you laugh at just to fit in. The opinions you soften so you don't seem "intense." The dreams you downplay because you don't want to make anyone uncomfortable. The parts of you that go dim every time you walk into a room built or someone else's identity, not your own.

It's not weakness. It's conditioning. You learned early that keeping the peace earns approval. That being agreeable earns closeness. That being low-maintenance earns praise. But at some point, those patterns stop being survival and start being self-abandonment. Most women don't notice when that shift happens. They just wake up one day realizing they've been living in a life that fits everyone but them.

Shift 3 is where that stops.

You start paying attention to what your body knows before your mind admits it: the tightness in your chest when you walk into a room that no longer feels aligned, the heaviness in your stomach when you're performing an outdated version of yourself, the relief you feel when you're finally alone and don't have to be "on" anymore. Those sensations are not random. They're signals. Invitations to stop forcing yourself into environments your future self already knows you've outgrown.

This isn't about burning your life down or cutting everyone off. It's about letting yourself expand *without asking permission* from people who benefit from your smallness. It's about understanding that outgrowing a room doesn't make you ungrateful—it makes you honest.

The rooms you've outgrown will not applaud your evolution. They will miss the version of you that made their lives easier. The girl who didn't ask for much. The girl who laughed off what hurt. The girl they could predict and depend on to stay the same. But you don't owe anyone the version of you that kept you invisible to yourself.

When you stop shaping yourself for rooms you've outgrown, you naturally rise into spaces where your fullness isn't just tolerated but expected. You attract friendships where your ambition isn't intimidating. You enter conversations where your voice feels grounded instead of swallowed. You stop settling for environments where your dreams feel like an inconvenience. You stop performing and start belonging.

And something profound happens when you finally walk into a room that can hold the real you: your body relaxes. Your ideas flow. Your voice steadies. You stop analyzing your every move and start trusting your presence. That's when you realize how heavy the old rooms felt. You didn't change into someone "too much." The space simply stopped fitting. This shift is also where your self-trust grows roots. When you stop needing every room to accept you, you realize belonging to yourself is the real foundation. You stop negotiating. You stop offering the world a version of you that doesn't feel genuine anymore. You start taking up space in your own life without waiting for approval.

Most women think their confidence problem comes from not being "good enough." Often, it comes from staying in environments that reinforce the smallest version of them. You can't expand in a room that only knows how to admire your past. You can't rise in a circle that depends on your predictability.

Shift 3 is where you choose spaces that can hold the woman you're becoming—even if that means walking out of rooms that have been part of your life for years.

It's not betrayal. It's alignment. It's not selfish. It's self-leadership.

The woman you're becoming doesn't enter rooms hoping to be accepted. She walks in knowing she gets to decide whether the room deserves her.

Shift 4: Stop Mistaking Control for Safety

It takes time, but every woman eventually sees it: the shield she thought she needed was the thing dimming her life. And for so many of us that shield is control.

Not the obvious kind—not calendars and color-coded to-do lists. The emotional kind. The instinct to predict outcomes so you're never caught off guard. The habit of scanning a room before you speak. The way you pre-plan conversations, rehearse your reactions, cushion your truth, soften your needs, and try to stay three steps ahead of disappointment.

We call it being responsible. Prepared. Self-aware. But most of the time, it's just survival dressed up as maturity.

Shift 4 is the moment you stop mistaking control for safety.

This shift asks you to look honestly at all the ways you've been gripping your life so tightly there's no room for anything new to reach you. The opportunities you didn't pursue because you couldn't guarantee the outcome. The relationships you held at arm's length because closeness felt unpredictable. The dreams you downsized because the bigger version required trust. The joy you muted because joy feels dangerous when you grew up waiting for the other shoe to drop.

Women who've spent years in survival mode don't always look anxious—they look prepared. Hyper-responsible. Hyper-attuned to what could go wrong. It feels like strength. It looks impressive. But underneath, it's exhaustion. It's fear. It's emotional bracing. It's the belief that you can only trust a life you can fully control.

That's where the real identity fracture lives—not in low confidence, but in low safety. Not in self-doubt, but in self-protection.

When control is in charge, everything becomes a negotiation. You don't take risks because risk requires surrender. You don't rest because rest requires letting go. You don't receive help because help requires vulnerability. You don't let yourself want something deeply because wanting makes you feel exposed.

Control convinces you that being unshaken is the same as being safe. But being unshaken is rigidity. Being safe is trust.

Control shuts the world out. Trust lets it change you.

Control is also one of the most socially praised forms of self-abandonment. People love the girl who handles everything. They admire the woman who never breaks. They applaud the one who doesn't need help, never loses her cool, keeps her life "together," and never asks for more than she's given. When everyone thinks you're fine, you stop remembering when you're not.

Shift 4 is the moment you stop performing stability and start choosing honesty.

It's admitting that predictability isn't peace—it's familiar discomfort. It's noticing how often your body is bracing for impact even when nothing is hitting you. It's feeling how tightly your shoulders, jaw, and chest have been holding it together because control convinced you tension was the same as protection.

It never was. It was just hiding.

When you release control, your power doesn't disappear—it returns. Real power isn't built on knowing every outcome. It's built on knowing you can handle whatever comes.

This shift asks you to revisit the parts of you that needed control in the first place: the girl who was called dramatic for feeling deeply, the teenager who learned everything fell apart if she didn't anticipate it, the woman praised for being strong and self-sufficient. She needed control. It kept her afloat. But you're not her anymore—and you don't need her survival strategies to build your next-level identity.

Shift 4 is where you begin to unclench. Not all at once, but one brave loosening at a time.

It's saying what you actually feel instead of what's safest to say. Letting yourself want something without immediately listing all the reasons it might not work. Allowing someone in, even when intimacy feels unfamiliar. Resting without guilt. Letting joy be joy instead of a threat. Trusting your intuition even when your old identity is begging you to overthink it.

When you stop mistaking control for safety, your life opens. Your relationships deepen. Your confidence becomes rooted instead of rehearsed. Your decisions get clearer. Your body relaxes. Your dreams finally have room to breathe.

Most importantly, you start to feel like someone you can trust.

Because trust isn't built by staying in control. It's built by letting yourself live—messily, honestly—without abandoning yourself in the process.

Shift 4 is where you stop gripping the steering wheel of your life so tightly your knuckles go white and finally understand you were never meant to control the road. You were meant to learn how to drive from trust instead of fear.

Shift 5: Reclaim the Voice You Silenced to Survive

You can feel it now, if you pay attention. It's that split second where something real comes up and you stop it. You know exactly what you want to say, but you don't. Your truth is right there, and you adjust it before it even leaves your mouth. It's subtle. Automatic. Easy to miss. But it's there, in the pause, in the edit, in the version of you that still chooses what's easiest to receive instead of what's actually true. And the more it happens, the more familiar it feels. You start reading the room before you read yourself. You start measuring your words against other people's comfort. And slowly, without even deciding to, your voice becomes something you manage instead of something you trust.

A silenced voice doesn't disappear, it redirects. It starts shaping how you think, how you respond, how you move through your life. Decisions feel heavier than they need to. You second-guess yourself more often. You begin living slightly out of sync with what you actually want, and over time, that disconnect becomes harder to ignore. Eventually, you feel it, like a buildup. A quiet tension when you're about to speak, decide, or choose. A hesitation that wasn't always there. A sense that something isn't fully landing, even when everything looks fine from the outside. That's the signal. Not something to push past, but something to pay attention to, because it's showing you exactly where you've been leaving yourself out and where you get to start choosing differently.

This is the shift where things stop living in your head and start showing up in how you move. You notice the moment you would usually hold back, and you don't. You say the thing. You stand by the decision. You let your truth exist without immediately adjusting it. Once you start responding from that place, your life begins to reorganize based on it. Your decisions get clearer. Your energy feels cleaner. You stop needing as much validation because you're no longer disconnected from your own voice. And over time, that becomes your new normal. You trust yourself faster. You move with more certainty. You stop abandoning yourself in the moments that used to define you. That's what this shift creates. Not a louder version of you, but a more self-led one. And once that's in place, everything else you build from here has a foundation that can actually hold you. This is where the where the real work begins.

Proof She's Real

You don't need to become a brand-new woman overnight. You just need to start noticing the proof that she's already here.

Everything you've just read in this chapter—the myths, the shifts, the way your identity has been running the show—was never about building a whole new you from scratch. It was about putting language to what's already been happening inside you.

Because the truth is, you've already been doing this work—in ways you didn't even realize. Every time you chose differently, every time you felt the fear and didn't fold, every time you showed up even when it didn't look perfect—that was her.

You've already had those moments. Tiny flashes of truth. Moments when you said something and shocked yourself. When you set the boundary. When you didn't over-explain. When you stood taller instead of apologizing for taking up space. When you caught yourself mid-thought and went, wait . . . that didn't feel like the old me.

That's identity work. Not a Pinterest quote. Not a mantra on your mirror. It's real. It's lived. And you've been living it, even in the quiet.

Look back for a second. Remember the time you said no and the world didn't fall apart. The moment you told the truth when it would've been easier to people-please. The day you looked in the mirror and, for a split second, didn't pick yourself apart—you just looked, and saw someone strong staring back.

That's her. That's proof.

It's easy to miss those moments because they don't come with applause. No one claps when you stop spiraling. No one cheers when you choose rest. No one sees the battle you win in your own mind when you stop talking yourself out of something you know you're meant for.

But you see it. You feel it. You live it.

Those are the moments that matter most—not the loud, shiny transformations the world celebrates, but the quiet ones you build when no one's watching. The nights you catch yourself before sending the apology text you don't owe. The mornings you decide to get dressed like a woman who respects herself. The afternoons you close the laptop, not out of laziness, but because you finally understand that rest is also discipline.

Every one of those moments is proof that she's real.

Maybe no one else has noticed yet. Maybe the world hasn't caught up to the version of you that's unfolding. That's okay. You're not doing this to prove anything to them. You're doing it because you're done proving and ready to be.

The work you've done to unlearn your old story—that's not small. The way you've started pausing before reacting—that's not small. The awareness you have now, the way you can feel when something's out of alignment—that's not small either. Those are shifts most people never even attempt.

So if you're sitting here thinking, *I still have so far to go*, I want you to hear this: you're already in motion. You're already doing it. You're already her.

Identity doesn't flip like a switch—it builds like muscle. And you're building strength every single time you back yourself.

Every time you hold your boundary. Every time you give yourself grace. Every time you stop apologizing for existing. Every time you choose honesty over performance.

That's what real confidence looks like. Not loud. Not flashy. Just consistent self-loyalty—practiced in private until it becomes who you are.

Maybe the old version of you still whispers sometimes. She'll say, *You're falling behind. You're messing it up. You're not doing enough.* That's okay. You don't have to fight her. You can thank her for trying to protect you—and then choose the new story anyway.

Because every time you choose differently, the old identity gets quieter. Every time you choose self-trust, the new one gets louder.

That's how identity shifts happen. Not through force. Through evidence. Through repetition. Through truth.

And the evidence is already all around you.

The woman you used to be wouldn't even be here reading this book right now. She wouldn't be curious about who she's becoming. She wouldn't be reflecting on her patterns. She wouldn't be open to the idea that she gets to rewrite her story.

But you are. That's not nothing. That's transformation in motion.

You've already stepped out of the old story simply by wanting something different. The desire for more isn't a sign you're ungrateful—it's a sign you're waking up. It's proof that the version of you you've been suppressing is ready to lead.

So take a second right now—really, right now—and think about the woman you're becoming. What does she already know that you keep forgetting? What does she already have that you keep pretending you don't? How would she look at you—at the way you're trying, the way you're still showing up—and say, "See? You're already doing it."

Because you are.

You don't have to wait for the big moment, the big break, the big sign. It's not coming to tell you you're ready. You've already been showing yourself that in a hundred little ways:

- When you stopped chasing someone's approval, that was her.
- When you finally spoke up in that conversation, that was her.
- When you said no without guilt, that was her.
- When you decided to go after something just because it felt right, that was her, too.

She's been with you this whole time. Not waiting at the finish line, but walking beside you, whispering, *Keep going. You're remembering me.*

That's the real truth of identity work—it's not about becoming someone new. It's about remembering who you were before the world told you who to be.

The woman you're becoming isn't an invention. She's a return.

And every decision you make from that place—every boundary, every truth, every act of self-loyalty—brings you closer to her.

You'll know you're there when peace feels normal. When silence isn't scary. When validation feels optional. When rest doesn't feel like guilt.

You'll know you're there when you stop asking yourself, *When will I finally become her?* because you'll realize you already are her.

That's the moment the story changes. That's the moment everything you've been practicing starts to click. You won't have to force it anymore. You won't have to prove it. You'll just be it.

And the world around you will start to respond differently, too. You haven't become someone else. You've simply stopped abandoning who you've always been. And this isn't just happening to you. This is happening everywhere. In women all over the world who are quietly taking their power back—one small, honest moment at a time.

There's the woman who used to say yes to everything because she was terrified of letting people down. The "nice girl" who built her identity on being agreeable, easy, and low-maintenance. Saying no used to make her stomach twist in guilt. The first time she let a call go to voicemail, it felt wrong. The first time she didn't volunteer, she worried people would think she was selfish. But she did it anyway. And nothing fell apart. Because saying no wasn't her being rude—it was her finally believing her needs mattered, too.

Then there's the woman who used to silence herself because she was told she was "too much." She learned to soften her voice, edit her fire, and play small to keep others comfortable. But one day she couldn't anymore. She wrote the post she'd been holding back. She said, "Actually, I don't agree." Her hands were shaking. Her heart was racing. But she did it. And in that moment, she remembered: her voice was never the problem. The room was just too quiet.

And then there's the woman who tied her worth to her work. The one who chased gold stars and burned herself out trying to earn her "enoughness." The overachiever. The doer. The one who thought rest was for people who hadn't earned it yet. When she didn't get the promotion, she realized what hurt most wasn't the rejection—it was that she didn't know who she was without the praise. So she started building a new story. One where her value didn't come from output, but from being. She stopped performing and started living. And for the first time, her peace felt more like success than any paycheck ever could.

These are the moments real women are living every day. That's the ripple effect of this work. Not just the loud wins, but the quiet reclamations. The micro-movements that say, *I remember who I am—and I'm choosing her now.*

> *You are not behind in life. You are not starting over. You are not lost. You are simply remembering your truth, one brave decision at a time. This is your proof. She's real. She's here. And she's you.*

As you turn to the rest of this book, that's only one thing I want you to carry with you: you're not trying to build her from scratch. You're learning how to trust that she's already inside you—and lead your life like that's the truth.

Key Points

If you strip everything back, this is what matters:

- Your life doesn't change when you feel ready. It changes when you stop abandoning yourself.
- The real shifts start in the small choices when you feel a pull toward something braver, bolder, and more aligned.
- Becoming the woman you want starts with noticing when you abandon yourself—and why.
- Confidence doesn't show up before the move—it shows up because of the move.
- You don't need to become someone else to feel confident. You need to stop abandoning the woman you already are.
- Your identity shifts through repeated, intentional choices that contradict the old narrative.
- You don't need to build a new you from scratch; you just need to trust that she's already inside you—and lead your life like that's the truth.

Chapter 2

The Identity Crisis You Didn't Know You Had

Before I ever understood identity, before I had language for self-trust, self-betrayal, or the quiet ways a girl learns to disappear inside her own life, there was a long stretch of time when I didn't recognize myself anymore. The loss itself was undeniable; it changed everything in an instant. But what came after didn't happen all at once. It happened slowly, quietly, in ways I didn't notice at the time. I didn't wake up one day and decide to become someone different. I adjusted, I adapted, and I learned how to move through my life in a way that felt manageable, even if it meant losing pieces of myself along the way.

Identity doesn't always announce itself. Sometimes it forms in the background while you're busy trying to survive something you never asked for.

When Survival Starts Pretending to Be Identity

After my mom died, the world felt split down the middle. There was the version of life everyone else was still living: the normal one, the busy one, the forward moving one. And then there was mine, suspended in a kind of emotional fog that wrapped itself around everything. Nothing made sense, but everything still demanded my attention. Teachers still talked. Friends still laughed. The clock kept moving at the same speed. And yet, I didn't feel like a person participating in any of it. I felt like a ghost trying to keep up with the living.

Grief at 15 doesn't look wise or poetic or profound. It looks like numbness you can't explain and exhaustion you can't justify. It looks like pretending you're okay because you don't have the language to tell anyone you're not. It looks like wanting someone to notice you're drowning, but also wanting everyone to stop looking at you altogether. It's contradictory and confusing and heavy in a way you don't understand until later, when you finally have the distance to see how much it shaped you.

I didn't know it back then, but that's when the earliest version of my identity started shifting—survival wrote the script for me. I started learning what the world seemed to reward: strength, silence, self-sufficiency. I learned that people were more comfortable when I didn't need anything. I learned that keeping myself together made everyone else feel better. I learned that if I acted fine long enough, maybe I'd start to believe it, too.

There's a particular kind of loneliness that takes root when you're praised for being strong during the worst moment of your life. Everyone means well when they say it. They think they're encouraging you. But what you hear—what I heard—is keep holding it in. Don't crack. Don't fall apart. Don't show too much. You're doing so good at pretending. Keep pretending.

So I did. I became the girl who hid her emotions. The girl who didn't voice her concerns. The girl who didn't need extra help. The girl who didn't talk about anything real. I didn't have the capacity to tell the truth about how I felt, so I figured out how to function without ever fully showing up. I learned to perform "okay" so convincingly that even I forgot there was another version of me underneath the performance.

This is the part of identity no one talks about: sometimes it begins with the smallest lies you tell yourself just to make it through the day. *I'm fine. I can handle it. It's not a big deal.* And the more you repeat them, the easier they are to believe. They start to feel true simply because they offer relief from what you're not ready to confront.

At that age, I didn't think about identity or future versions of myself or any of the concepts I teach now. I just thought about getting through the next hour. The next class. The next conversation where I hoped no one would ask me how I was doing. I didn't want to talk. I didn't want to explain. I didn't want to be the girl whose mom died. I just wanted to feel normal, even if it meant hiding every part of myself that didn't fit into the illusion.

But surviving comes with a cost. The more I pushed everything down, the more disconnected I became—from myself, from my emotions, from the life I was still supposed to be living. I started losing track of what I wanted or how I felt. I didn't trust myself to speak up. I didn't trust myself to be vulnerable. I didn't trust myself to need anything at all. Because needing felt dangerous. Needing felt exposed. Needing felt like it might unravel me completely.

Looking back now, I can see that I wasn't just grieving my mom. I was grieving myself. The version of me that felt light. The version of me that didn't second-guess everything. The version of me who knew how to ask for help because she hadn't learned yet that people leave. When you lose someone that central, that foundational, you don't just lose the person—you lose the part of you that felt safe being soft.

And once softness feels unsafe, silence becomes a personality. Self-sufficiency becomes identity. Emotional endurance becomes a skill you don't even realize you're mastering. Everyone around me saw strength. But it wasn't strength. It was survival—packaged neatly, delivered quietly, and applauded loudly enough that I kept performing it long after I needed to.

This is where identity conditioning really begins: in the moments where you start choosing the version of you that offends the least. The girl who doesn't take up space. The girl who doesn't complicate anything. The girl who doesn't ask for more than the bare minimum because she's afraid even that might be too much.

I didn't know it then, but those early months after my mom died were building the foundation for the identity I'd carry for years. The one in which I believed I wasn't smart enough. The one in which I believed I wasn't capable. The one in which I believed that disappearing a little made everything easier.

And this is the part that sets up everything that comes next: once you start shrinking yourself in one area of your life, it becomes easier to shrink everywhere.

The classroom. Friendships. Romantic relationships. Opportunities. Dreams.

Every space that required me to show up as myself felt threatening. Every situation that required me to be seen felt impossible. I didn't have the language for it then, but now I can name exactly what was happening: I was building an identity on being invisible because invisibility felt safe.

But identities built on survival don't come with an expiration date when you're living inside them. They feel permanent. They feel factual. And the more moments that reinforce them, the deeper they root themselves into how you see yourself.

For me, that realization didn't come all at once. It didn't even come in a moment of clarity. It came in a classroom—one ordinary afternoon that wasn't supposed to mean anything. One comment from a teacher that wasn't meant to wound as deeply as it did. One split second when every quiet insecurity I had been carrying finally demanded to be heard.

Because that moment didn't just hurt. It marked me. It shaped the identity I carried into adulthood. And it became the script I would spend years learning how to rewrite.

The First Script I Didn't Know I Was Writing

I can look back now and see exactly when it happened—the moment the first identity script quietly took root. It happened in a classroom that smelled like dry erase markers and stale winter air. It happened on a day that looked ordinary to everyone else but felt impossible to me. And it happened months after losing my mom, at a time when the world had already decided I should be "better" by now.

Grief does something strange when you're young. At first, it's loud. People hover. They check in. They give you space, casseroles, soft looks. But the world moves on quickly, and teenagers move on even faster. Eventually, everyone goes back to math tests and weekend plans, while you're still waking up every morning to the same empty house, the same aching quiet, the same reminder that nothing will ever be normal again.

When the noise faded, the silence hit harder. I didn't know how to explain that I wasn't sleeping, that I couldn't focus long enough to read a sentence, that I was living inside a body that felt like it had been unplugged from itself. So I didn't. I just pretended. Pretended I was functioning. Pretended I was coping. Pretended I was still the same girl, even though I felt like a ghost wearing her clothes.

That pretending became its own kind of exhaustion—one that didn't show up on my face but screamed inside my chest. Everything felt foggy. My brain, my days, my memories, my sense of time. I wasn't "acting out." I wasn't rebellious or dramatic. I was drowning quietly. And the quieter I became, the easier it was for everyone to believe I was fine.

One afternoon, I was sitting at my desk staring at a worksheet I couldn't make sense of. My binder was half open, papers stuffed into pockets that refused to close, a test I hadn't finished shoved underneath a textbook I hadn't opened. I was doing everything I could to stay unnoticed—chin down, pencil moving just enough to look busy, hoping no one would ask anything of me.

And then I heard my name.

"Alicia," my teacher said, irritation already threaded through his voice. "Do you have the answer?"

My entire body froze. My mind went blank. I knew I should have had the answer, but I didn't even know what chapter we were on. Time slowed in the way it only does when you're terrified of being exposed. Every head turned toward me. Every inch of my skin felt hot. I could feel my heartbeat in my throat.

"I . . . I don't know," I whispered.

The sigh he let out still echoes somewhere inside me. It wasn't just disappointment—it was annoyance. Judgment. Confirmation of everything I already feared might be true. He said something about paying attention, something about trying harder, something that made the whole class look at me like I was the problem.

I remember staring at the desk, trying not to cry, trying not to breathe too visibly, wishing I could disappear into the floor. It wasn't embarrassment. It was shame. Heavy, sticky, immediate shame. Shame that told me I wasn't just struggling—I was failing. That I wasn't just grieving—I was falling behind. That I wasn't just having a hard year—I wasn't smart enough to keep up anymore.

I didn't have the language then to understand what was happening to me. I just knew something inside me sealed shut. A quiet promise formed—the kind of promise that feels protective in the moment but becomes poisonous over time.

Don't get noticed. Don't try too hard. Don't give anyone the chance to call you out again.

That single moment became the blueprint for a whole identity. I didn't choose it consciously. That's the thing about identity scripts—they don't introduce themselves. They creep in silently and settle into the parts of you that are most tender. At 15, I didn't understand that my brain was just trying to keep me safe. I didn't understand trauma or shutdown or cognitive overload. I just thought something was wrong with me.

So I shrank. I stopped raising my hand, even when I knew the answer. I stopped turning in assignments, even when I had half-finished them at home. I stopped showing up as a participant in my own life and became a shadow instead. And the more I pulled back, the more the world confirmed the story I'd begun telling myself: you're not capable. You're not enough. You don't belong here.

And eventually, that identity caught up to me in a way I couldn't ignore. I stopped trying altogether. I stopped caring about school. I stopped believing it was a place I belonged. And before I fully understood what I was doing, I dropped out.

At the time, it didn't feel like a big, defining moment. It felt like relief. Like stepping away from something I had already convinced myself I wasn't capable of anyway. But looking back now, I can see it clearly, it wasn't just a decision. It was confirmation. Proof of the identity that had already started to take shape.

When people talk about identity, they imagine dramatic turning points. But most identities are formed in moments exactly like this—micro-moments that feel small to everyone else but huge to you. A comment, a look, a sigh, a mistake that gets magnified in your mind until it becomes a trait. Not "I didn't know the answer" but "I'm not smart." Not "I froze in class" but "I'm someone who disappoints people." Not "I'm grieving" but "I can't handle life."

Looking back now, with the clarity of adulthood, I can see the truth that 15-year-old me couldn't: nothing about that moment was about capability. It was about *capacity*. I wasn't behind—I was heartbroken. I wasn't lazy—I was grieving. I wasn't stupid—I was overloaded. But when you're young, no one explains that your brain can shut down under emotional weight. They just expect you to push through it.

And so, without realizing it, I internalized that moment as evidence. Evidence that I shouldn't try. Evidence that failure was inevitable. Evidence that the safest way to survive was to stay small and unnoticed.

That's what identity scripts do—they become the quiet rules you live by without ever questioning where they came from.

Years later, I still had a version of that teacher's sigh living in my body. Still had that classroom heat rising in my face anytime I didn't understand something immediately. Still had that instinct to make myself invisible anytime I felt even slightly out of place. I didn't connect the dots then, but now I can see how often I made choices from that 15-year-old identity instead of the woman I actually was.

That's the danger of early identity scripts. They don't fade on their own. They grow with you. They get louder every time life hands you another moment that feels even a little bit similar. They become the narrator in the background, whispering things that sound like truth only because you've repeated them so long they feel familiar.

But familiar and true are not the same thing.

It took me years to understand that the shame I carried wasn't a reflection of who I was—it was a reflection of a moment my nervous system misread as identity. That classroom didn't define my intelligence. It defined how I protected myself. And once protection becomes identity, it becomes hard to imagine anything else exists.

This is why I bring you into this memory. Not for sympathy. Not for storytelling. But because identity scripts don't announce themselves; they slip in silently during moments when you were too overwhelmed to defend yourself. And unless you see them clearly, you keep living from them long after the moment has passed.

That day in the classroom was not about a math or history problem. It was about the first time I believed the lie that shrinking would keep me safe. That not trying was better than trying and failing. That disappearing hurt less than being seen and misunderstood.

And that belief, the quiet, unspoken one, didn't stay in that moment. It carried into the choices I made after it. The way I pulled away. The way I stopped showing up. The decision to leave school altogether. And from there, it followed me into adulthood, shaping how I moved through relationships, opportunities, and every space that asked me to be seen. It became the script I didn't know I was reading from. Until one day, much later in life, I finally realized I wasn't living as me—I was living as the girl who froze at her desk and decided never to risk being wrong again. That was my first identity fracture. And naming it now is what finally made it lose its power.

What Happens When an Old Identity Leads

There's a strange thing that happens when a moment from your past becomes the narrator of your present. You don't notice it at first. You just assume this is who you are now. You assume the habits you formed in survival mode are personality traits. You assume the caution you carry is maturity. You assume the shrinking you do in certain rooms is just being "polite." You assume the way you overthink everything is just how your brain works. You never stop to consider that maybe—just maybe—you've been living from a version of yourself that no longer exists.

That's what an old identity does. It stays in charge long after its job is done.

I just showed you where it started for me, now I want to show you what happens when you don't even realize you've been living from a script you never meant to write. Because that high school classroom moment didn't just leave me feeling small that day—it shaped the years that followed. And that's exactly how it works for so many women. One moment becomes a rule. One scar becomes a personality. One survival instinct becomes an identity. And then you wake up one morning, years later, realizing the woman running your life is a girl who was just trying to keep herself from falling apart.

When an old identity leads, everything becomes filtered through a version of you that was formed when you didn't have the capacity to understand what was happening to you.

As you grow up, the script grows with you. Not noticeably. Not aggressively. Quietly. In the decisions you don't make. In the dreams you don't speak out loud. In the opportunities you talk yourself out of because something in your chest whispers, *Be careful. Don't get it wrong. Don't be too visible. Remember what happened last time.*

The truth is, identity doesn't freeze you in place—it moves you without you realizing it. It shapes how you interpret the world, how you respond to discomfort, how you make choices, how you love, how you work, how you speak, how you silence yourself, and how you try to protect yourself. And unless you learn to question the identity you inherited, you will keep living inside a story you don't even remember choosing.

For me, that old script showed up everywhere. I didn't walk into rooms thinking, *I'm not smart enough.* I walked in feeling it. Feeling it in the way my shoulders curled inward. Feeling it in the way I avoided eye contact. Feeling it in the way I tried to make myself as easy to ignore as possible. No one was judging me. But my body still reacted as if I were in danger of being seen unprepared. That one classroom moment trained me to assume that visibility meant exposure. That exposure meant risk. And that risk meant shame.

So I became someone who excelled at flying just under the radar. Not too loud, not too ambitious, not too demanding. I got good at being the girl who didn't ruffle feathers. Who didn't draw attention. Who didn't give anyone a reason to look too closely. I thought I was being humble. I thought I was being responsible. I thought I was being realistic about "who I was." But really, I was just living from a girl who had decided that disappearing was safer than disappointing anyone again.

And this is where most women start to see themselves in my story—not in the details, but in the pattern.

Maybe your script wasn't written in a classroom. Maybe it was written at a dinner table where emotions weren't welcome, so you learned to swallow yours whole. Maybe it was written in a relationship where your needs were "too much," so you learned to never ask. Maybe it was written in a childhood home where conflict felt dangerous, so you learned to bend yourself into whatever shape kept the peace. Maybe it was written in a workplace where your ideas weren't taken seriously until someone else said them, so you learned to play small even when you knew you were capable of more.

Whatever the moment was for you, the pattern is the same: you start organizing your whole life on staying safe, not staying true.

Old identities aren't loud. They don't shout. They whisper. They nudge. They convince. They disguise themselves as practicality, as caution, as *this is just how I am*. They show up in the hesitation before you speak. In the apology before you say no. In the guilt that hits you after doing something just for yourself. In the exhaustion that comes from performing stability for everyone around you. In the numbness that creeps in when you're living a life that looks fine but doesn't feel like home.

You think you're just tired. You think you've just changed. You think this is adulthood, or motherhood, or womanhood. You think you're being responsible, grounded, reasonable. But what's actually happening is that an outdated identity is still making your decisions for you, and you don't even realize it.

Women don't lose themselves all at once. They lose themselves slowly, by degrees. In the moments when they convince themselves something doesn't matter. In the moments when they prioritize everyone else's comfort over their own truth. In the moments when they feel a spark of desire and immediately smother it with logic or fear. In the moments when their voice rises in their throat but stays behind their teeth. In the moments when they feel the nudge to change direction but decide to "be grateful" instead of being honest.

That's the old identity talking. That's the survival version of you thinking, *Stay here. Stay safe. Don't rock anything. Don't risk anything. We know this place. We know how to survive here.*

Except you're not trying to survive anymore. You're trying to become. And becoming requires a different narrator.

But before you can change the narrator, you have to understand how much of your life she's been writing:

- **Old identities sneak into your relationships.** You start choosing partners based on who makes you feel safe in your smallness instead of who makes you feel seen in your fullness. You choose friendships in which you play the helper or the listener but never the one who gets messy or needs support. You keep people close who reinforce the version of you you're secretly trying to outgrow because the unfamiliar feels threatening.
- **Old identities sneak into your goals.** You find yourself dreaming in miniature. You lower your ambitions so they don't feel dangerous. You choose paths that guarantee predictability instead of ones that guarantee fulfillment. You avoid rooms you know you're meant for because the old script still says you're not qualified.
- **Old identities sneak into your self-talk.** You criticize yourself with phrases that sound like you but belong to someone else. You say things like "I'm just not good at that," "I'm too much," "I'm not enough," "I can't trust myself," not realizing those sentences were written by a younger, scared version of you who was doing her best with what she had.
- **Old identities sneak into your joy.** You feel guilty when life feels good. You brace for impact. You prepare for loss before anything has even happened. You don't let yourself enjoy what you've built because it doesn't match the identity that expects everything to fall apart.
- **Old identities sneak into your voice.** You water down your opinions. You repeat the socially acceptable version of your truth. You choose silence when your whole chest is begging to speak. You have something to say. But the identity that learned "being small is safer" is still in charge. The hardest part is that none of this looks traumatic from the outside. It looks functional. It looks polite. It looks responsible. It looks like

> someone who has her life together. That's why it's so hard for women to realize they're living an identity crisis—they're not falling apart. They're performing their life so well that no one, not even themselves, can see the disconnect.

You don't have to be at rock bottom to be misaligned. You just have to be living a life that feels slightly too small for you—and pretending you don't notice.

When I talk about identity work, this is the part most women finally exhale. Because they realize the reason they've felt stuck has nothing to do with laziness, or lack of discipline, or "not being confident enough." It has everything to do with an identity that was shaped without their consent, leading a life they've long outgrown.

And once you see it—really see it—you can't unsee it. You start noticing the tiny ways you choose safety instead of truth. You notice the quiet moments when your body reacts before your mind does. You notice the internal tug-of-war between the girl who learned to stay small and the woman who's dying to expand.

This is where the real awakening happens. It shows up in the micro-moments when you catch yourself doing something automatic and think, *Oh. That's not me. That's the old story.* You notice the apology that slips out before you've even done anything wrong. You notice the invitation you decline because you don't trust yourself to be seen. You notice the dream you dismiss because it feels "too much." You notice the way you brace yourself before giving an opinion. You notice the way your stomach tightens when you disappoint someone. You notice the resentment that builds after yet another "sure, I can do that" you didn't want to say yes to. You notice the guilt that flares up when you rest. You notice the joy you cut short because it feels unfamiliar.

These aren't personality quirks. These are identity scripts. These are the inherited rules you live by without realizing it. These are the ways the old narrator keeps control.

But here's the most important part: the moment you begin to notice them, the narrative starts to shift. Awareness breaks the trance.

Your old identity can't lead as powerfully once you've seen how it operates.

This doesn't mean the feelings go away overnight. It doesn't mean the old thoughts vanish. It doesn't mean you suddenly wake up bursting with confidence. Identity work isn't a glow-up montage. It's a process of choosing who leads your life now: the girl shaped by survival or the woman shaped by truth.

When an old identity leads, you live small. When a new identity leads, you live awake.

This is the part of the journey when you don't have to fix anything—you just have to see it. See the patterns. See the stories. See the conditioning. See how many of your decisions have been made from protection, not possibility.

This section—this inner seeing—is the bridge between who you've been and who you're becoming. Because you cannot embody a new identity while living in alignment with an old one. You cannot build a life that feels alive while following rules that were written in a moment of fear.

And once you know that, once you feel it click in your chest the way it finally clicked in mine, you realize something that changes everything: you were never broken. You were living from a version of you that was never meant to stay.

And now you get to choose differently.

The Architecture of a Good Girl

There's a reason your identity feels heavy in your hands: it wasn't built by accident. It was constructed quietly, piece by piece, long before you ever had words for what was happening. Women don't wake up one day disconnected from themselves. We are shaped into it. Trained into it. Praised into it. Conditioned into roles we never consciously agreed to play, but learned to perform because the world applauded us when we did.

Every woman has been handed a blueprint at some point—not an instruction manual exactly, but an invisible architecture of who she's supposed to be. Be agreeable. Be sweet. Be grateful. Be low-maintenance. Be easy. Be responsible. Be quiet when it's inconvenient for others. Be everything for everyone but never too much for anyone.

No one says these things directly. They don't have to. We absorb them the same way we absorb language, through repetition, through reward, through example from our mothers and the women we grew up watching, and through the subtle shifts in someone's face when we show too much or want too loudly.

Who you become is decided in the moments that feel ordinary. And almost every woman has lived inside some version of the "good girl architecture," even if she didn't know that's what she was building. See if any of these archetypes resonate:

- There's the **easy girl**, the one who learned early that the fastest way to belong was to require nothing. She doesn't make waves. She doesn't ask for much. She keeps the peace even when she's crumbling inside. People adore her because she never pushes back, never complicates things, never asks anyone to look at themselves. But inside, she's exhausted. She's resentful. She's starving for someone to care for her the way she cares for everyone else. She's been trained to believe that needing nothing makes her lovable—and she's terrified to find out what happens when she finally asks for something she actually wants.
- Then there's the **chill girl**, the one who learned to swallow disappointment like it's a personality trait. She acts unbothered because being passionate or expressive was called dramatic. She acts "whatever works for you" because having preferences was labeled "too much." She learned to keep her energy low so the people around her wouldn't feel pressured to rise. But the truth

is, she was never chill—she was careful. And the real her isn't low-maintenance. She's low-expectation. A girl who learned that wanting anything too deeply made her vulnerable to losing it.

- There's the **achiever girl**, the one who mistook performance for worth. She learned early on that praise came when she excelled, not when she existed. So she kept overachieving until burnout felt normal and rest felt dangerous. She became fluent in checklists and accomplishments. She built her self-worth like a résumé. And even when she hit the milestones, she never felt different inside—because the girl building them still believed she had to earn the right to feel proud. These women grow into adults who don't know how to stop climbing because they've never been taught how to stand still without feeling useless.
- There's the **peacemaker girl**, the one who learned to mediate, soften, smooth over. She can read a room better than she can read herself. She can sense tension before anyone else notices it. She knows how to defuse a situation before it explodes—but she does it at the cost of her own needs. Her nervous system has been trained to scan for danger, not desire. She thinks she's being helpful, but really she's just performing emotional labor she never agreed to carry. If you put her in a room where no one needs her, she doesn't know who to be.
- There's the **caretaker girl**, the one who was taught—explicitly or not—that her role is to hold everything together. She remembers birthdays, plans the reunions, checks in on everyone else, and makes sure nothing falls apart. She holds the emotional glue of every group she's in. But no one asks who holds her. No one asks who checks on the strong one. Her identity becomes holding—holding the pieces, holding the peace, holding the weight of everyone else's lives until her own life feels secondary.

- There's the **good daughter**, the one who followed every unspoken rule—don't be a burden, don't take up space, don't disappoint, don't want anything too big. Her adulthood becomes one long performance of the girl she thought she needed to be to stay loved. She grows into a woman who avoids conflict at all costs, even when it costs her connection.
- There's the **good partner**, the one who gives and gives and gives until she is running on fumes. She thinks love means absorption. She thinks compromise means self-erasure. She thinks being nurturing means abandoning herself. She has no idea that love is supposed to be reciprocal because she grew up believing she had to earn the right to be chosen.
- There's the **strong one**, the woman who never breaks, never asks for help, never lets anyone see her softness. She learned that vulnerability was risky, so she became invincible instead. But strength without support is just isolation disguised as resilience, and eventually she realizes she built a life in which no one ever gets close because she never lets them.

Each of these roles is different, but they all come from the same place: survival. We don't choose these identities because they're weak. We choose them because they worked. They kept us safe. They kept us accepted. They kept us loved—or at least kept us from losing love.

But at some point, the architecture becomes a cage. The blueprint becomes too tight. The roles become unsustainable. And the woman you're becoming starts to push against walls that were never meant to hold her in the first place.

Over time, this truth becomes impossible to ignore:

The identity you built to survive cannot be the identity you live inside forever. What kept you safe as a girl will suffocate you as a woman.

That's why you feel restless. That's why you feel disconnected. That's why you feel like you're performing instead of living. You are simply outgrowing the roles the world taught you to play.

This is when you realize that the architecture wasn't built for your becoming. It was built for your compliance. It was built to keep you predictable, agreeable, palatable, manageably small. It was never designed with your expansion in mind.

Identity work begins the moment you decide to step out of those inherited roles and ask the question no one ever taught you to ask: *Who am I when I'm not performing the version of me that makes everyone else comfortable?*

That's when the real transformation begins. Because you stop trying to be the easy girl, the chill girl, the achiever girl, the caretaker girl, the peacemaker girl, and you start becoming the woman who was buried underneath all of them.

You start honoring your preferences. You start trusting your desires. You start choosing truth over peacekeeping. You start letting people carry their own discomfort. You start letting your voice reenter the room. You start letting yourself take up space: emotionally, physically, spiritually, unapologetically.

And the more you do that, the more the old architecture cracks. The more the blueprint becomes irrelevant. The more your identity becomes something rooted in who you *are*—not who you learned to be.

Identity in Action

When I left the Yukon, I didn't magically step into a new version of myself. I didn't walk out of that life and suddenly feel healed or whole or ready for anything bigger. What happened instead was slower, quieter, more human. I went back home to Saskatchewan and started piecing myself together in the most ordinary ways. Sitting on my bed with my journal, writing things I didn't want to admit, catching myself in old patterns, and choosing something different in moments no one else would ever see. It wasn't Instagram-worthy. Some days felt like progress, some days felt like nothing at all. But it was the first time in years that I wasn't abandoning myself just to keep the peace.

And somewhere in the middle of all that rebuilding, Brent came into my life.

It didn't feel overwhelming. It felt safe in a way I didn't fully understand yet. He showed up consistently, in a way I wasn't used to. He loved me without conditions, without questions, without needing me to shrink or perform or earn it. And that felt unfamiliar. Not confusing or chaotic, just different. When you've spent years questioning everything, being cared for like that doesn't instantly change you. It takes time to let it in, to stop questioning it, to believe it's real. Those first two years with him changed me. *Being loved steadily brought something into the light I hadn't fully faced yet—how deeply I still struggled to love myself.* It showed me where I still hid. Where I still settled. Where I still didn't trust my own voice. My life was more stable than it had been in years, but I still felt like I was holding back in ways I couldn't fully explain.

The thing about identity work is that it doesn't show up with instructions or clarity. It shows up in the small ways you start choosing yourself differently, even when no one's watching. And for me, that shift started long before any big move. It began in the mornings when I didn't talk myself out of wanting more. It lived in the nights when I let myself imagine a version of life that wasn't built on survival. It stretched in the moments when I didn't silence myself just to stay agreeable. Those were the early signs. The quiet recalibrations. The proof that my identity was already shifting, even if I didn't have the language for it yet.

And then came the decision that changed everything: moving to the West Coast.

It wasn't impulsive or reckless. It was clarity. A deep, internal knowing that staying where we were would keep me circling the same version of myself I had spent 2 years trying to outgrow. Saskatchewan had been my home most of my life, the place that held both my deepest pain and the pieces of me that survived it. It was somewhere I could land, but never somewhere I could fully become myself. Something in me knew I needed different surroundings if I wanted to become the best version of myself.

And Brent felt it, too. He didn't push. He didn't question. He simply said, "Then let's go," the way someone does when they truly love you.

We had a plan. Boxes packed, everything starting to come together, both of us knowing we were about to start something new on the coast. And right as it was all lining up, something came in that we hadn't planned for. It wasn't what we expected, and it made us stop for a second and really look at what was in front of us. Not chaos. Not crisis. Something bigger. Something that felt like a plot twist and a promise at the exact same time.

A few days before we were supposed to pack the car and head west, something felt off. Not in a scary way. Just enough that I couldn't ignore it. Everything around me felt chaotic, but I felt weirdly still. And somewhere in the back of my mind, I had a feeling I couldn't quite explain. When the test turned positive, I remember just sitting there, staring at it. No big reaction. Just silence. Like my brain needed a second to catch up. And underneath it all, there was this quiet feeling that this moment mattered more than I could fully understand yet. That's when it hit me: I was pregnant. And even though I hadn't planned for it, it didn't feel out of place. Maddie wasn't just the most incredible surprise of my life, she was a turning point. The kind of truth that enters your life exactly when you're finally brave enough to grow into the woman who can hold it.

And so, with that new reality pulsing through me, we packed the car anyway. We chose the life we wanted anyway. We drove west anyway.

Because identity shifts don't wait for perfect timing—they meet you in the middle of your becoming and dare you to trust yourself even more deeply than you did the day before.

Identity work doesn't wait for stability. It asks for truth. It asks for self-trust. And that drive west was the first time I realized I was finally leading my life instead of letting fear lead it for me.

When we arrived on Vancouver Island, everything felt unfamiliar. Boxes half-open. Salt in the air. A new life stretching wide and undefined. Nothing was decided yet—how we'd build our life, what the next chapter would look like—but for the first time in my whole life, the unknown didn't feel threatening. It felt exciting. It felt like a place where the real version of me might finally have room to breathe.

A few days later, I walked down to the beach near our new place. It was one of those cold, gray days, a little windy, nothing special. The tide was out, and everything just felt . . . open and quiet. I sat there for a long time, knees pulled to my chest, jacket zipped to my chin, listening to the waves roll in and out. Everything in my life was uncertain. Our rental wasn't unpacked yet, I still needed to find a doctor or midwife and I had no idea what the future would look like. But for the first time, I didn't feel lost.

I felt . . . free.

I looked out at the water and placed my hand over my stomach. *We're going to be okay*, I whispered. *And something in me settled when I said it.* I didn't have proof. Nothing about it looked stable. But in that moment, I realized I had finally stopped abandoning myself. I wasn't the girl waiting for someone to save her anymore. I wasn't the one running back to what was familiar, even when it hurt. I wasn't trying to earn worth through struggle or pain.

For the first time, I trusted me.

The waves kept moving, the seagulls circled overhead, and I just sat there—watching, breathing, letting the fear settle into something softer. I thought about everything that had led me here: leaving the Yukon, packing up my life, walking away from what was supposed to be my forever. Every decision that felt impossible, every sleepless night, every time I chose the unknown over what was easy.

That's what identity work actually looks like in real life. Not the polished version of a new chapter. It's not the glow-up montage. It's sitting on a cold beach, pregnant, terrified, and somehow still sure that you're exactly where you're meant to be.

I didn't have a clear plan for what came next. But I knew this: I wasn't going back. Not to the old patterns. Not to the smaller version of me who mistook control for safety. Not to the identity that said, "You'll only be okay when everything's perfect."

Because that day, sitting by the ocean, I realized something deeper: peace isn't found in control. It's found in trust.

That's what identity work builds. Not perfection. Not endless confidence. Trust. The kind that lives in your body. The kind that whispers, *You can handle this*, even when your mind is screaming, *But how?*

I didn't know how I'd build a life here. I didn't know who I'd become yet. But I knew I was done living as a woman who doubted herself more than she believed in herself.

And that knowing—small, quiet, unshakable—was the start of everything.

When I stood up to leave, the wind pushed against me, cold and strong, but it didn't knock me over. It felt like a reminder. That I could stand here, unsteady and still okay. That I could be scared and still certain. That I could build a life on that kind of faith.

As I walked back to the car, the world felt lighter. The fear was still there, but it wasn't in charge anymore. Because for the first time, I wasn't letting the old identity lead. *I was leading me.*

This chapter wasn't just about awareness—it was about authority. Because the stories you've been living out? You didn't choose them. But you can rewrite them. You can catch them mid-sentence. You can flip the script. You can show up as a new version of you—starting now.

That's what identity work is. It's not aesthetic. It's not affirmations. It's how you lead yourself—especially when your old self tries to sneak back in.

So here's your permission slip, if you need one: you don't need to earn the new identity. You don't need to wait for proof. You don't need anyone else to see it before you do. Start seeing her now. Because she's already here. She's already in you. And you get to decide, today, to live like that's the truth.

You're Not Broken, You're Conditioned

If there's one thing that I want you to hold onto from this chapter, it's this: the version of you who learned how to survive deserves to be understood, not judged. She did what she knew how to do. With what she had. In the environment she was in. Those patterns weren't flaws. They were protection. They were intelligence. They were how you made it through.

Every belief you've carried wasn't born from your flaws. It was born from the environments you lived in, the expectations you absorbed, the stories handed to you before you even knew you were allowed to question them. You learned to be the good girl, the strong one, the easy one, the responsible one, the one who held it all together. Not because you chose those roles, but because they were the safest ones offered to you.

That doesn't make you broken. It makes you human.

Your identity didn't fall apart because you're weak—it blurred because you were never taught how to separate who you *really* are from who you were trained to be. And most women don't even realize it's happening until they wake up one day, look around at a life that "makes sense," and feel that quiet ache of misalignment humming underneath everything. That ache isn't failure. It isn't a flaw. It's your truth tapping on your shoulder saying, *Hey. . . I'm still here.*

When you look back on the girl who built all these old identities—the one who held her breath in classrooms, who kept the peace at dinner tables, who smiled through pain because no one seemed to notice she was hurting—you realize she wasn't weak at all. She was resilient. She was resourceful. She was doing everything she could to keep going without the language, support, or emotional safety she deserved. She wasn't doing something wrong. She was doing her best.

And you're still doing your best. You just finally have enough awareness to see where you've been living on autopilot.

What you've called *overthinking* is often just the part of you that learned she couldn't afford to make mistakes. What you've labeled *people-pleasing* is often the part of you that learned love felt conditional. What you've judged as "being too emotional" is often the part of you that learned expression came with consequences. These aren't character flaws—they're echoes. Old patterns trying to keep you safe in new seasons of your life.

But you're not in those old rooms anymore. You're not that version of you anymore. And that means you don't need those rules anymore.

This chapter wasn't about dissecting your past. It was about giving language to something you've felt for years but couldn't quite name—that strange mix of exhaustion, numbness, responsibility, and restlessness that makes you wonder, *Why don't I feel like myself?* That's not brokenness. That's misalignment. That's the friction between an old identity trying to hold on and a new one trying to emerge.

And here's the part most women don't hear enough: the moment you see your conditioning clearly, the spell breaks. You can't unsee it. You can't cram yourself back into the smaller version of you just because it's familiar. Awareness isn't the end of the journey—but it *is* the beginning of real freedom. Once you understand why you've been living the way you have, everything starts to shift. You don't force this shift. It starts the moment you realize you're allowed to.

> *You're allowed to question the rules you were raised with. You're allowed to want more than survival. You're allowed to outgrow roles that once kept you safe. You're allowed to build an identity rooted in truth instead of trauma. You're allowed to stop apologizing for the woman you're becoming.*

You've already done the hardest part—you've woken up to yourself. You've looked at the patterns you've been carrying and said, *This isn't mine anymore.* You've seen where your life was built on old expectations instead of real desire. And now you're here, reading this, because something in you knows it's time. Time to stop waiting. Time to stop shrinking. Time to stop rehearsing an identity built for a girl who had fewer choices than you do today.

Identity conditioning isn't a life sentence. It's just a starting point. The moment you start choosing differently, the moment you start trusting yourself over the scripts you inherited, the entire trajectory of your life shifts.

You are not too late to become the woman you can feel yourself growing into. You were conditioned—and now you're conscious. Which means you're *damn* powerful.

Key Points

If you're taking anything with you, take this:

- Once you start shrinking yourself in one area of your life, it becomes easier to shrink everywhere.
- When an old identity leads, everything becomes filtered through a version of you that was formed when you didn't have the capacity to understand what was happening to you.
- The real awakening happens in the micro-moments when you catch yourself doing something automatic and think, *Oh. That's not me. That's the old story.*
- You cannot build a life that feels alive while following rules that were written in a moment of fear.
- The identity you built to survive cannot be the identity you live inside forever. What kept you safe as a girl will suffocate you as a woman.
- Identity work does not build perfection or endless confidence; it builds trust—the kind that lives in your body.
- There is nothing wrong with you.

Chapter 3

Why You're Still Playing Small (Even Though You Know You're Meant for More)

Life didn't suddenly become perfect after that day on the beach. But something about it became more real than it had ever felt before. I noticed it in the everyday things: ocean air through the windows, baby lotion on my hands, waking up beside someone who made me laugh before I'd even had coffee. For the first time in years, my life didn't feel like something I was desperately trying to hold together. It felt like a life I was living.

The Life I Wanted, the Me I Lost

Life on the island was simple in the best way, and it held a kind of peace I hadn't seen coming. The mornings felt slower. The nights were louder. And in between, life just felt . . . fuller. It was everything I used to sit and think about when I was back in Saskatchewan, wondering if things would ever feel different.

A few months after the move, Maddie arrived—my bright blue-eyed girl with a giggle that cracked me open in places I didn't know were still closed. She came into the world with her *baba*'s spirit and this little spark in her eyes that felt like a reminder: life wasn't done surprising me.

Motherhood didn't hit me all at once. It came in waves I was trying to figure out in real time. Moments of love that felt almost overwhelming, mixed with quiet thoughts like, *Can I actually do this?* I didn't have a perfect plan. I didn't have some strong, polished version of myself ready to step into the role. I just had a baby girl who looked at me like I was her whole world. And somehow, even in my uncertainty, that was enough.

Then, only six months later, life threw me another plot twist: two pink lines. Rhett. I remember sitting on the bathroom floor, test in hand, laughing and crying all at once while Maddie babbled happily in her swing. I was stunned—equal parts terrified and amazed—realizing I was about to become a mom of two under two. Our babies would be only 15 months apart. I used to think chaos was something to avoid. Now it was woven into the fabric of my days: beautiful, messy, heart-stretching chaos that grew me in ways I didn't see coming.

Those early years felt like a blur of being needed. Sleepless nights, bottles scattered across the counter, laundry multiplying behind my back, tiny hands reaching for me from every direction. My days were full, my heart was fuller, and still, underneath it all, there was this quiet hum I couldn't name. Not unhappiness or regret. Just the feeling that somewhere along the way, I had started disappearing inside the life I had fought so hard to build.

It's strange how growth works. You spend years climbing your way out of survival mode, building a life you once only knew how to imagine, and then—once you finally get it—you realize you still have to build yourself inside it. Stability doesn't erase old patterns. Joy doesn't automatically restore lost parts of you. Even beautiful lives can make you forget your edges when you're trying so hard to hold everything together.

I was deeply happy. Truly. Motherhood stretched me in all the ways it does. But there was also this quiet kind of tired underneath it all. Something I couldn't explain, something that didn't go away just because life looked good on the outside. Some mornings I'd wake to tiny hands patting my face and think, *This is the dream. This is what I prayed for.* And moments later, a softer truth whispered under my ribs: *So why do I still feel a little bit lost?*

I tried telling myself it was normal. That motherhood changes you. That identity shifts are part of the deal. But deep down, I knew this wasn't just about becoming a mom. There was something in me that still didn't feel settled yet.

And that brings me to *that* morning.

It was a regular Wednesday—ordinary, unremarkable, forgettable in every way except the one that mattered. I stood barefoot in the kitchen wearing the same pajamas I'd slept in, hair piled on top of my head like it was protesting the whole situation, kids zooming around the living room as if they had somewhere very important to be. The dishwasher hummed behind me. Cartoons chattered in the background. A faint scent of burnt toast clung stubbornly to the air. A diaper sat in the garbage, unbothered and definitely overstaying its welcome. Vanilla and baby wipes had become my new signature scent.

It was all so normal. And maybe that's why it hit me so hard—because it's in the normal that women disappear the quietest.

I looked at the clock: 10:07 a.m. My coffee had been reheated three times and still sat untouched. The dishes piled up in the sink, and I let them. I didn't have the energy to care. I caught a glimpse of my reflection in the oven door—hair frizzed, skin pale, shoulders slightly slumped—and thought, I'll shower later. There's no point right now.

But that one thought wasn't innocent. It was a trapdoor.

Why bother putting on makeup? Why get dressed? Who am I even getting ready for?

The questions slid in quietly, disguised as practicality. But underneath them was something I recognized too well: self-abandonment wearing the mask of "it's fine."

Because I'd been here before—maybe not in this kitchen, but in this energy. The version of me who only showed up when someone was watching. The woman who believed effort was only worth it if it benefited someone else. The girl who thought joy, beauty, and personal expression were luxuries she had to earn. That old identity was back—moving through my house like she still lived there.

I could feel her in the slump of my shoulders, the heaviness in my eyes, the silent resentment that didn't have a name. I could feel her in the way I was half-living, waiting for someone to tap me on the shoulder and remind me I mattered, too. It's a strange and painful thing to recognize your own disappearance.

And then I looked at Maddie. She was sitting on the floor surrounded by crayons, hair wild, smile wide. She glanced up at me with pure pride on her face, holding up her artwork like it was the greatest masterpiece ever created. And in that moment, I saw the woman I wanted her to see when she looked at me. Not this tired, dimmed-down version who kept putting herself at the bottom of the list, always waiting for some future moment where she'd finally get to feel alive again.

The realization hit hard enough to crack something in me open. *I wasn't just abandoning myself—I was teaching her how to do it, too.* Not through words, but through modeling. Through the way I kept postponing myself. Through the way I only showed up fully when people were around to witness it. I was showing her a version of womanhood I didn't believe in. And the thought of her mirroring that one day broke me.

So I did something tiny. But tiny things have power when you've been disappearing.

I turned on music. Loud. The kind that makes you remember who you were before life got so damn serious. I wiped the counter—not to look productive, but to create space. I grabbed clean clothes. I stepped into the shower.

And I didn't rush it. For the first time in a long time, I let the hot water hit my skin like it was rinsing off more than just the night. I blow-dried my hair. I put on the self-tanner, the mascara, the bronzer, the blush. I sprayed the perfume that had been collecting dust.

Not for anyone else. Not because I had somewhere to be. Not to impress anyone.

But because it made me feel like me again.

The me who used to take herself seriously. The me who moved with intention. The me who didn't wait until life felt "easier" to show up fully. The me who existed before survival mode became a lifestyle.

As I stood in that same kitchen, now smelling faintly of freshly washed hair and perfume instead of burnt toast and stale coffee, something softened inside me. I realized this is what becoming her looks like. Not in big, cinematic turning points. Not in perfect timing. Not in dramatic declarations.

It happens in the middle of your ordinary life. It happens when no one's watching. It happens when you stop abandoning yourself in small, forgettable moments. It happens when you remember that your identity doesn't need permission to exist.

Nothing external changed that morning. The dishes were still piled up. The kids were still loud. The house was still messy. But *I* changed. I made a decision—a quiet one, but a life-altering one.

I chose me.

And not in a selfish way. Not in a dramatic "new chapter" kind of way. In the simplest, most human way possible: I stopped treating myself like a background character in my own story.

Becoming her starts like that—with one act of self-loyalty. One moment when you stop waiting for permission. One small decision that reminds you who you are underneath all the responsibility and noise.

That morning didn't fix everything. But it reminded me I was still in here. It helped me find the thread back to myself—the one I promised I would follow all the way home.

And this time, I meant it.

Why You're Still Playing Small (Even Here)

The strange thing about finally getting the life you once prayed for is that you assume the shrinking will disappear with it. You think the version of you who used to doubt herself, negotiate her needs, read the room too closely, and make herself easier to hold will naturally fall away the minute life starts to feel safer. You expect confidence to rise with happiness. You expect steadiness to arrive with stability. You expect that once the pain lessens, the old patterns will quietly pack up and leave with it.

But that is rarely how it works.

For most women, playing small was never some random flaw in their personality. It was never just low confidence or a lack of boldness or some unfortunate character trait they were born with. It was a learned strategy. A way of staying connected, accepted, protected, chosen, and emotionally safe in environments where being fully expressed did not always feel possible. It was adaptation. It was intelligence. It was your system paying attention and making decisions based on what helped you survive with the least amount of loss.

That is why these patterns can stay alive long after the circumstances that created them have changed. Because your life can move forward faster than your conditioning does. Your environment can shift. Your relationship can soften. Your home can become safer. Your opportunities can expand. Your world can become bigger, healthier, more stable, and more beautiful than it has ever been. And still, some old part of you can keep responding as if the original rules are still in place.

That is the part so many women do not understand at first. They think if life is good, they should automatically feel different inside it. They think safety should instantly create confidence. They think love should erase hesitation. They think a better chapter should produce a better identity all on its own. But the body is not that quick to update. The nervous system does not revise itself overnight just because your circumstances improved. It stays loyal to what once worked. It stays familiar with what once felt safest. It keeps reading from the script it learned in the season when shrinking felt like wisdom.

So even here, even now, even in a life you genuinely love, some part of you may still be reacting to old information.

You may still soften what you really mean before it leaves your mouth. You may still hesitate before asking for what you need. You may still feel yourself bracing when attention lands on you for too long. You may still instinctively make your wins sound smaller, your opinions sound gentler, your desires sound more reasonable, your needs sound less demanding. The desire for more is real. So is the older pattern still trying to keep you within the boundaries of what once felt emotionally survivable.

That is why playing small can be so confusing in this season of life. It does not always look like insecurity in the obvious sense. Sometimes it looks like being agreeable. Thoughtful. Self-aware. Mature. Flexible. Accommodating. It can look like being the easy one. The understanding one. The low-maintenance one. The woman who does not ask for too much, take up too much, need too much, or reveal too much too quickly. On the surface, it can all look socially acceptable. Even admirable. But underneath it, the same old pattern may still be running: stay contained, stay manageable, stay safe.

And because those patterns are often rewarded, they can live in you for years without being questioned. The world often praises women for being easy to accommodate. For being agreeable. For keeping the peace. For swallowing discomfort with grace. For making themselves digestible. What began as adaptation starts to feel like identity. It starts to feel like personality. It starts to feel like "just who I am."

That is part of why this chapter matters. Because you cannot change a pattern you still mistake for yourself.

The truth is, a lot of women are not lacking desire. They are not lacking dreams. They are not lacking depth, intelligence, insight, or longing. They know there is more in them. They can feel the tension of it. They can sense the life that wants to be lived more honestly. What gets in the way is not the absence of desire. It is the presence of conditioning that still whispers caution every time truth asks to take up more space.

That whisper can show up in all kinds of ordinary ways. In the pause before you speak. In the way you rehearse a text before sending it. In the way you downplay what you really want so no one can accuse you of wanting too much. In the guilt that rises when you choose yourself without cushioning the choice in enough explanations. In the need to manage how your joy lands on other people. In the way you instinctively prepare for disappointment even in moments that are meant to feel good. In the reflex to scan for what could go wrong the minute something starts going right.

That does not mean you are broken. It means your body has memory.

Your system remembers when visibility created friction. It remembers when honesty changed the mood in the room. It remembers when wanting more made you harder to understand, harder to love, harder to hold. It remembers what it cost to be too direct, too emotional, too bright, too excited, too disappointed, too disappointed again. And even if your mind now understands that you are no longer in the same environment, your body may still be treating old experiences like current instructions.

That is why good things can still feel uncomfortable sometimes. That is why stable love can make you brace. That is why peace can feel unfamiliar. That is why joy can come with a strange edge of tension. Because part of you is still more practiced in managing struggle than receiving goodness. Part of you still trusts the familiar ache more than the unfamiliar ease. Part of you still believes that being fully alive might cost more than it is worth.

And that is why playing small can continue even when your life has outgrown the pattern.

It is not because you secretly want less. It is not because you are incapable of change. It is not because all your healing meant nothing.

It is because some part of you is still organized on survival in a season that is asking for truth.

That conflict creates a very particular kind of inner friction. One part of you knows what feels true now. One part of you can sense what your life is asking of you now. One part of you is tired of living half-expressed, half-contained, half-available to your own depth. And another part is still answering to rules that were written years ago. Rules about being careful. Being easy. Being unthreatening. Being grateful for what you have and quiet about what you still want.

That is why hesitation can feel so loaded. It is rarely just about the moment in front of you. It is the collision between old loyalty and present truth. Old protection and current possibility. Old self-preservation and the life you are actually standing in now.

Once you understand that, you stop personalizing every moment of resistance. You stop turning hesitation into evidence that you are not ready. You stop making your slowness mean you are failing. You stop reading every instinct to shrink as proof that something is wrong with you. Instead, you begin to see the pattern for what it is: a learned response that once made sense, still feels familiar, and no longer deserves to lead.

That is the real shift in this section. Not forcing yourself into a bolder performance. Not trying to shame yourself into confidence. Not pretending the fear is gone. Just understanding the mechanism well enough that you stop confusing conditioning with truth.

Because once you can see that clearly, the question changes.

It is no longer, *Why am I like this?* It becomes, *What old rule is still trying to run this moment?*

It is no longer, *Why can't I just be different already?* It becomes, *What part of me still believes shrinking is the safest move?*

And when you start asking that better question, you create the possibility for a different answer.

What It's Actually Costing You

The cost of playing small is not always obvious at first. That is part of what makes it so easy to live with for so long. It does not always show up as some dramatic crisis or some visible collapse that forces you to confront it all at once. More often, it shows up quietly. Gradually. In the subtle erosion of your self-trust, your clarity, your sense of aliveness, and your connection to yourself. It shows up in the way life can look full from the outside and still feel strangely hard to inhabit from within.

This is the kind of exhaustion many women carry without knowing how to name. The kind that has very little to do with how much is on their plate and everything to do with how little of themselves they are actually bringing to their own lives. It is the tiredness of chronic self-editing. Of overriding what you feel. Of filtering what you say. Of managing how you are perceived. Of softening what is true so no one else has to feel too much in response to it. That kind of exhaustion does not always announce itself loudly. Sometimes it just hums beneath the surface of your days until you start mistaking it for normal.

And that is where the deeper cost begins.

Because every time you override yourself, something in you registers it. Every time you swallow your truth to keep things smooth, every time you downplay a desire because it feels inconvenient, every time you talk yourself out of what feels honest because it might create friction, some part of you is learning a lesson. Not the lesson you want it to learn, but one all the same. It learns that your truth is negotiable. That your needs can wait. That your instincts are not necessarily to be trusted. That your inner world is something to edit before it can be lived.

At first, those moments can seem small. Harmless, even. A softened opinion here. A swallowed no there. A decision to not make it a big deal. A habit of staying quiet until the moment passes. But they accumulate. And over time, repeated behavior starts to feel like identity simply because it has become so familiar.

That is one of the deepest costs of smallness: it trains you out of clear self-trust.

You begin to lose your own signal in the noise. Your instincts get harder to hear. Your desires become foggier. Your opinions become easier to second-guess. You stop knowing, in a clean and immediate way, what you actually feel because you have spent so long adjusting those feelings before they ever fully land. Instead of hearing yourself clearly, you start running yourself through layers of interpretation. Is this too much? Is this fair? Is this selfish? Is this worth it? Am I overreacting? Am I asking too much? Am I making this harder than it needs to be?

That mental loop is expensive.

It takes energy to constantly manage yourself. It takes energy to keep your reactions measured, your needs softened, your joy moderated, your disappointment contained, your desires explained away before anyone can challenge them. It takes energy to live in a state of ongoing self-correction. And because so many women have been doing that for years, they no longer recognize how much of their vitality is being consumed by it.

That is why this kind of tiredness can feel so confusing. You can be doing everything right on paper. Taking care of your responsibilities. Showing up for the people you love. Handling your work. Checking the boxes. Building a life that once felt impossible. And still feel drained in a way that sleep does not solve. Still feel disconnected in a way rest does not fully reach. Still feel like something in you is underfed, underused, underexpressed.

Because the issue is not always volume. Sometimes the issue is disconnection.

When you keep living from a shape that is too small for who you are, life starts to lose some of its color. You can feel it in the dulling of joy. In the way excitement gets cut off at the knees by overthinking. In the way spontaneity gives way to carefulness. In the way desire begins to feel impractical instead of alive. In the way your life becomes something you manage efficiently rather than something you inhabit honestly.

That is a real loss.

It affects more than your happiness. It changes your relationship with yourself. You stop trusting yourself with the life you actually want. You start assuming you are too inconsistent, too overwhelmed, too easily discouraged, too sensitive to disappointment, too likely to backslide. So, you stop wanting things fully. You stop naming them cleanly. You stop letting yourself imagine them without immediately attaching conditions. Maybe later. Maybe when things calm down. Maybe when I feel more ready. Maybe when I know I can follow through.

That is how smallness steals possibility.

It does not usually stop you from wanting more. It just makes it feel safer to stay vague than to commit. Safer to hold back than to hope. Safer to maintain what is familiar than to risk the emotional exposure of fully showing up for what you know you want.

And the longer that pattern continues, the more it can affect your sense of aliveness. Because aliveness requires presence. It requires contact with your truth. It requires the freedom to want, feel, choose, and respond without constantly filtering yourself through old fear. When every decision gets run through caution, performance, and self-protection, something in you starts to flatten. Not all at once. But enough that you begin to feel it. Enough that you start wondering why your life looks good but does not always feel as rich as you thought it would.

This is what playing small can cost over time:

- Your ability to hear yourself clearly
- Your trust in your own responses
- Your willingness to want things fully
- Your capacity to feel deeply present in your own life
- Your connection to the parts of you that make life feel vivid, honest, and yours

And maybe that is the part that hurts most. Not simply that you hold yourself back, but that you begin to lose touch with yourself in the process. You become less reachable to your own truth.

Less available to your own voice. Less connected to the woman inside you who knows exactly what feels aligned and what does not.

That is why this conversation matters.

Because this is no longer just about confidence. It is no longer just about speaking up more or showing up more boldly or finally taking up space.

It is about whether you are willing to keep paying for old protection patterns with your self-trust, your aliveness, your clarity, and your connection to your own life.

And once you see that clearly, the conversation changes.

The pattern is no longer just something you tolerate because it feels familiar.

It becomes something you begin to tell the truth about. Something you measure differently. Something you stop romanticizing as humility or maturity or self-control. Something you recognize as expensive.

That recognition is powerful.

Because the moment you stop minimizing the cost, you stop treating the pattern like a harmless quirk. You start seeing it as a real form of loss. And once you can see the loss clearly, something in you begins to resist it. Something in you begins to understand that the life in front of you deserves more of you than this. That you deserve more of you than this.

That is where the shift begins.

Not in shame. Not in judgment. Not in forcing yourself into a new personality.

But in finally telling the truth about what staying small has been taking from you.

What Expansion Looks Like (in Real Life)

Expansion rarely feels the way people expect it to feel. Most days, it feels like an interruption to the life you were already moving through. A subtle pull. A flicker of something new. A quiet invitation that shows up in the middle of an otherwise ordinary day and asks something different from you.

It looks like you standing in your kitchen, wiping crumbs off the counter you've already wiped three times, feeling a tug inside your chest that whispers, *You're shrinking again.* It looks like catching yourself saying yes when every cell in your body wants to say no. It looks like scrolling past your own reflection in the mirror and feeling that familiar ache—*I miss me.* Not the old you. The real you. The one who hasn't had space to breathe in a while.

Expansion lives in those small moments. The ones no one else notices. The ones that don't look heroic from the outside. The ones that feel inconvenient, ill-timed, or almost embarrassingly subtle. But these moments matter because this chapter of your life isn't about dramatic reinvention; it's about remembering. Reclaiming. Re-expanding into the woman you keep glimpsing but haven't given yourself permission to be consistently.

> *You don't expand by wishing for a different life. You expand by showing up differently inside the one you already have.*

Expansion is deciding to pause before you automatically dim your excitement in a conversation because you're afraid someone will roll their eyes. It's catching the impulse to downplay your wins and choosing—just once—to let yourself speak the truth without shrinking it. It's closing your eyes for three slow seconds before responding to a message because you know the old you would reply out of guilt, obligation, or fear, and the real you deserves a different pattern.

Expansion doesn't sound like, "I've completely changed my life." It sounds more like, "Not this time."

Not this time I won't cancel on myself. Not this time I won't swallow my words. Not this time I won't treat my desires like they're optional. Not this time I won't choose the version of me who's easier for everyone else.

> *This is how self-trust is rebuilt—not through giant leaps, but through monumental micro-moves.*

It's you walking into your closet on a random Tuesday and putting on the outfit you've been "saving" for some imaginary moment when you feel more confident. It's ordering the meal you want instead of the one that looks disciplined. It's leaving the dishes for 10 minutes so you can stand in the sun and remember you exist outside of your roles. It's the text you send without over-explaining. The boundary you set without apologizing. The way you let your voice stay steady even when your heart is pounding.

It's unfiltered. It's intimate. It's deeply personal. And it is powerful.

Because every time you choose yourself in those tiny, inconvenient moments, your body receives proof that you can be trusted. And proof is what rewires your identity—not affirmations, not motivation, not waiting for the stars to align. Proof.

This is what I watch happen with women all the time. They come to me saying, "I feel stuck. I know what I want. I just can't seem to move." And they think the answer is confidence. Or discipline. Or some magical bolt of readiness.

But every single time, the shift begins in a place they never expect: a micro-decision.

Like the client who told me she couldn't take the leap because she didn't feel ready. She wanted to wait until she felt more qualified, more healed, more sure of herself. I told her what I learned the hard way—that readiness isn't a feeling. It's something you build in motion.

She didn't change her life by doing something dramatic. She didn't quit her job or move across the country or wake up one day fearless. She started doing extremely small things extremely differently. She put on lipstick again—not for a date or an event, but because it made her feel alive. She took five minutes to sit in silence before scrolling. She said no to something she'd usually say yes to just to avoid disappointing someone. She let herself want what she actually wanted instead of editing it down to be more reasonable.

And one day, she emailed me: "I didn't need a new life. I just needed to stop abandoning myself in this one."

That's the essence of expansion. Not reinvention—reconnection. Not chasing a different life—inhabiting your current one from a completely different level of self-loyalty.

You don't need to blow up your world. You don't need a dramatic rebirth. What you need is to stop performing the smaller version of yourself who's been leading out of habit. What you need is to stop living on autopilot inside a life that needs *you* in it—not the filtered, digestible version of you, but the full one.

Expansion looks like this: it's recognizing the exact moment you're about to dim and choosing one inch more truth. It's noticing your instinct to soften and choosing one inch more presence. It's feeling fear tug at your sleeve and choosing one inch more courage anyway. Fear is still there, but it no longer gets the final say. It's letting yourself take up 5% more space today than you did yesterday. Not 50, not 100, just 5. That's enough. That's how you build a life that feels aligned instead of managed.

And each time you choose that 5%, your life rearranges itself around your new standard. People will respond differently—not always comfortably, but honestly. Opportunities start to feel closer. You become someone who follows through because your identity now includes self-loyalty, not just survival. Your days feel less like something you're getting through and more like something you're participating in.

You'll feel it first in your mornings: the way you breathe differently, the way you move slower, the way you meet your reflection without bracing. Then you'll feel it in your relationships: the conversations that feel more honest, the boundaries that feel cleaner, the space you create by not filling silence with explanations. Eventually, you'll feel it in your energy: the subtle shift from *I hope I can do this* to *I know who I am.*

This is what expansion looks like in practice: less performance, less self-abandonment, and more of you present in your actual life, making choices that align with the woman you know you're meant to be. Every woman you admire—the ones who move with ease, the ones who seem grounded no matter what, the ones who are quietly magnetic—didn't become that way by waiting for confidence. They became that way by practicing micro self-loyalty until it became their identity.

And the same is available to you. Not someday. Not when life slows down. Now. Today. In the tiny choice right in front of you. Because expansion isn't a moment. It's a practice. A practice of returning to yourself, over and over, *until the return becomes your home.*

This Is When You Decide

There is always a moment before the visible moment. A split second when your body reaches for the familiar before your mind has fully caught up. You feel it in the hesitation. In the urge to smooth what you were about to say, soften what you were about to do, or reach for the version of yourself that feels easier to manage. It happens quickly. Quickly enough that most women move right past it without ever realizing it was there. They tell themselves they are being polite. Mature. Easygoing. But often, what looks like composure is really self-abandonment happening in real time.

That split second matters more than most people realize. It is the point when your old conditioning meets the truth of who you already are. No one else in the room may notice it. But internally, something real is happening. A pattern is either being repeated or interrupted. A familiar reflex is either being reinforced or challenged.

This moment can show up any time, usually in the breath before you choose between what feels true and what feels familiar. It is subtle enough to miss, but important enough to shape your life.

This is where identity becomes real. Not when you think about changing. Not when you journal about it or promise yourself tomorrow will be different. Identity becomes real in the moment when your nervous system reaches for the familiar and you decide whether you are going to follow it automatically or stay present long enough to choose on purpose.

Most women have lived inside these patterns for so long they no longer recognize them as patterns. What began as adaptation starts to feel like personality. And because so many of these habits are socially rewarded, they can go unexamined for years.

That is why this work can feel subtle and confronting at the same time. Because the moment itself is often small, but what it reveals is not. It reveals who has been leading. It reveals what you still believe you need to do in order to belong. It reveals how quickly you are willing to leave yourself when approval feels uncertain.

The old identity is practiced. She knows how to smooth, soften, explain, apologize, and make herself easier to hold. She knows how to keep you acceptable. She knows how to keep your desires contained inside a life other people can tolerate. She has survival skills. She has history. She has had years of repetition. And because she has been in charge for so long, she can feel like you.

But she is not the whole of you.

There is also a truer part of you. A steadier one. The part that does not move from panic. The part that does not scramble for approval. The part that does not over-explain her no or dilute her yes so that it lands more gently for everyone else. The part that is no longer willing to organize her life based on who might be uncomfortable if she were fully expressed. She is not trying to become someone else. She is simply no longer available for the negotiations that require her to leave herself behind.

And this is the real work. Not forcing yourself to become fearless. Not performing confidence. The real work is learning how to stay with yourself in the moment where your old identity wants to take over. It is noticing the pull toward smallness and deciding, sometimes with shaking hands, that it does not get to lead this time.

These moments may not look impressive from the outside. But they are the moments that rebuild self-trust in the body. Because self-trust is not rebuilt through ideas alone. It is rebuilt through lived evidence. Through the moment you tell the truth and remain standing. Through the moment you stop editing yourself and realize you are still safe on the other side of that choice. Through the moment you let your own voice stay intact.

This is your training ground.

This flicker. This hesitation. This space between instinct and action. This is where the work leaves the page and enters your life. This is when everything you say you want gets tested in the smallest and most revealing ways. Because it is easy to say you want to trust yourself. It is much harder to do it in the middle of an ordinary moment when your old habits are asking for one more turn at the wheel.

That is why willingness matters more than readiness.

Readiness is often just another way of delaying the choice. Willingness says, *I may still feel the pull of the old identity, but I am no longer handing her every decision. I do not need to feel fully confident to choose differently. Even here, even now, I can stay with myself.*

The women who expand are not always the women who feel the readiest. They are the women who become willing to interrupt the pattern. Willing to pause in the middle of the familiar reflex. Willing to ask what is most true here, and then answer honestly.

So, the question is not whether you are ready. The question is whether you are willing. Willing to notice the flicker. Willing to pause before the old pattern closes over the moment. Willing to stop calling self-abandonment maturity. Willing to choose in favor of your own truth, even when no one else sees the effort it takes.

Because this is where you decide.

Not later. Not when life calms down. Not when you have more certainty, more evidence, or more time. Here. In the ordinary moments that seem too small to matter, but actually matter most. In the breath before you override yourself. In the pause when your old identity reaches for the familiar and your truth asks for something different.

This is when you decide who leads.

When I Stopped Shrinking

It didn't happen in some perfectly timed aha moment that looked pretty on paper or like the ones you see in the movies. It happened in the middle of my real, messy, ordinary life—when the kids were finally asleep, the house smelled faintly of leftovers and baby shampoo, and the only sound in the kitchen was the steady hum of the fridge.

I was standing at the sink, hands submerged in warm, soapy water, staring at the wall in front of me completely zoned out. The dishes weren't the problem. The exhaustion wasn't the problem either. It was the heaviness behind it—the kind that doesn't lift with sleep, caffeine, or a good cry. The kind that comes from performing a version of yourself that isn't real anymore.

That night, for the first time, I let myself say the truth out loud: I'm not tired because I'm doing too much. I'm tired because I've been disappearing in the doing. I'd spent so many years surviving, being the strong one, the steady one, the one who held everything together that I didn't realize how much of myself I'd filtered out in the process. The performance was subtle—smiling when I didn't feel okay, softening my opinions, rushing through my own needs, pretending I didn't want more than the quiet, safe version of life I'd built.

And the wildest part? From the outside, it looked like everything was fine (again). Better than fine. I had the family. I had the home. I had the stability I used to beg the universe for. But inside, something was slipping. Not drastically—just quietly. A loosening of color. A dimming that didn't happen all at once, but little by little, moment by moment, until I realized I'd become a background character in the very life I'd worked so hard to create and rebuild.

It hit me like a soft truth, not a harsh one: this isn't burnout. This is misalignment. This is what it feels like to live the life you wanted, but not fully live *in* it.

Standing there with my sleeves rolled up, my reflection faint in the window behind me, I finally understood something I had been avoiding—readiness wasn't coming. I had been waiting for confidence, clarity, time, energy, validation, a sign . . . but all that waiting was fear dressed up as patience. I kept telling myself I'd start healing deeper once things settled, once I felt more like myself again, once

I had a better grip on everything. But the waiting was the very thing keeping me stuck.

I leaned against the counter, tears slipping quietly down my face, and let myself feel it instead of outrunning it. Not the earth-shattering sadness—just the honest grief of realizing how long I'd been holding my breath.

And that's when the truth landed: I couldn't white-knuckle my way into becoming the woman I wanted to be. I couldn't mindset my way out of years of self-abandonment. I couldn't journal my way through wounds that were still living in my body. And I definitely couldn't expand into a new identity while using the same survival strategies that were designed to keep me small.

I needed support. Real support. The kind that helps you rebuild from the inside instead of patching over the cracks. The kind that holds you while you unravel and teaches you how to put yourself back together without losing the parts you like. The kind that reminds you that healing isn't a sign of weakness—it's a sign of self-respect.

It wasn't the kind of scene you'd frame. It didn't feel like a bold, empowered move. It felt raw. Vulnerable. Necessary.

So I did something I had avoided for years. I dried my hands. I walked to my bedroom. I sat on the edge of the bed with my phone in my shaky hands. And I made the appointment.

I was finally ready to stop pretending I had to do it all alone. Because if I was truly going to become the woman I kept writing about in my journal—the one who trusted herself, the one who didn't shrink, the one who could hold her own life with both hands—I needed help becoming her. Not the Instagram version of healing. The real thing.

When I pressed "confirm," it felt like a hinge. A door opening. A quiet but powerful yes to myself. And that decision—the smallest, scariest, most honest choice—became the moment everything in my life started to shift again. Not instantly. But deeply.

That's the part no one talks about: living as the woman you are meant to be is not about being strong. It's about being willing to stop shrinking long enough to let yourself be supported.

Key Points

You don't need to remember everything. Just take these points with you as you move forward:

- Becoming your true self starts with one act of self-loyalty. One moment where you stop waiting for permission. One small decision that reminds you who you are underneath all the responsibility and noise.
- The world you're navigating now requires a different version of you—one who leads instead of hides, one who trusts instead of doubts, one who shows up without shrinking.
- Every time you silence your needs, you reinforce the idea that your desires are inconvenient.
- When your life becomes one long performance of who you think you're supposed to be, you lose access to who you truly are.
- The expanded version of you doesn't need you to be fearless. She just needs you to be honest.
- Every time you choose differently, you create evidence that you can trust yourself.

Part One

CLOSER AND REFLECTION

Part One Closer: The Truth That Sets You Free

If you've made it this far, you already feel it—the quiet shift happening inside you. Not the loud "new chapter" moment the world loves to celebrate, but the deeper kind. The kind that happens when you finally see your life, your patterns, and your identity with honest eyes. The kind that lifts a weight you didn't know you were carrying.

Part One wasn't about fixing anything. It wasn't about forcing a glow-up or creating a whole new version of you. It was about naming what's been true for a long time: you've been living from an identity that was built for survival, not expansion. You've been moving through a life that looks good on paper, while quietly wondering why you still feel like something is missing. You've been showing up for everyone but yourself, carrying roles you never consciously agreed to, repeating patterns you outgrew years ago.

And now? You see it. You see the moments you've been shrinking without realizing it. You see the ways you've abandoned yourself in the name of being easy, agreeable, low-maintenance, dependable. You see how tired you are—not from doing too much, but from doing too much of what pulled you away from who you actually are. Awareness isn't always comfortable, but it's liberating. Once you see the truth, you can't go back to pretending you don't.

And that's the gift of this part of your journey: you finally understand why you've felt stuck, why you've dimmed your voice, why you've played small even when you knew you were meant for more. It was never because you weren't capable. It was because you were conditioned. You were protecting yourself. You were surviving.

But survival isn't your ceiling. And now that you can see the old identity clearly, you're no longer ruled by it.

Part One ends here. There's no big breakthrough or neatly tied bow, just something far more powerful: readiness. Not the kind you wait for, but the kind you claim. The kind that rises inside you when you realize you don't need to earn a new identity—you just need to stop abandoning the one that's been whispering for years, *Let me lead.*

You've met the truth. You've seen the patterns. You've named the exhaustion for what it is. And now you stand at the doorway of something new—not a reinvention, but a return. A return to self-trust. A return to honesty. A return to the version of you who doesn't shrink, doesn't apologize for wanting more, and doesn't postpone her life until she feels "ready."

Part Two is where you meet her. The woman you've been sensing in the background. The one who feels grounded, steady, certain—even when life isn't perfect. The one who leads from truth instead of fear. The one who trusts herself in a way you haven't felt in years. She's not a fantasy. She isn't far away. She's the woman you become when you stop negotiating with your old identity and finally choose yourself.

You've walked through the truth. Now it's time for what comes next.

Becoming her. Now.

Part One Reflection: Come Home to Yourself

Before you move into the next part of this book, take a moment and breathe. You've just walked through the truth of who you've been, where she came from, and why those old identities felt so familiar. You've seen the patterns. You've heard the echoes. You've remembered parts of yourself you didn't realize you were still carrying. None of that is small. None of that is accidental. And none of that is the whole story.

This is your pause. Your exhale. Your moment to stop rushing, stop bracing, and let yourself actually feel what's shifting inside you. You don't have to force anything here. You don't have to already "be better." You just have to tell the truth to yourself—maybe for the first time in years.

As you sit here, ask yourself these questions gently, honestly, without judgment. Let whatever rises be enough.

- What version of me have I been loyal to—even when she was quietly hurting me?
- Where have I been shrinking out of habit, not truth?
- What part of me is ready to stop waiting for permission and start telling the truth of what I actually want?

These questions aren't meant to diagnose you or give you homework. They're mirrors—small, clear, and honest. They show you who you've been, but, more importantly, they reveal what's waking up inside you.

Now choose one micro-action—just one—that aligns with the woman you're becoming. Not a big decision. Not a life overhaul. Just a simple, self-loyal act you can do today. Maybe it's changing out of the clothes you've been wearing out of convenience. Maybe it's saying no to something you say yes to out of reflex. Maybe it's buying the perfume you've been saving for a special occasion and deciding today is the occasion. Whatever it is, let it be small, doable, and honest.

You don't need a perfect plan. You just need one moment where you stop shrinking and start choosing yourself.

And as you close this part of the book and step into the next—the part where we shift from knowing to becoming—carry this with you:

I am allowed to choose myself now.

Because you are. And when you do, everything changes.

Part Two

BECOMING HER NOW

You've made it through the part of the book where people usually stop. It takes a level of honesty most aren't willing to sit with. But you did that. You let yourself name what's been holding you back. You let yourself see the patterns, the shrinking, the places where you've been surviving instead of living. And now you're standing in the doorway of something completely different.

This is where everything begins to shift. You understand what's been shaping you, and you can move differently because of it. You're not trying to "fix" yourself anymore. You're not hunting for confidence like it's a prize someone else hands you. You're not trying to become a shinier, better, more disciplined version of the woman you were before. You're learning how to trust yourself again. You're learning how to return to yourself. You're learning how to build a life that fits you from the inside out.

Part One cracked the shell. Part Two is where you step out of it. This section isn't about reinventing your entire life or burning everything to the ground. It's not about becoming an entirely new woman overnight. It's about the version of you who already exists—buried under years of conditioning, survival mode, and silence—and bringing her forward, piece by piece, choice by choice, moment by moment.

This part is about doing the work in real time. Not in theory. Not in quotes you save on Instagram. In your actual, everyday life—when your kids or anyone and anything in your life needs you at the same time your needs tap you on the shoulder, when you wake up not feeling like *her* at all, when doubt sits in the back row of your mind whispering its old lines. This is where you learn to choose differently anyway.

You're not here to perform your healing. You're here to live it.

Chapters 4–6 walk you into self-trust, not as a feeling, but as a practice. They show you what embodiment looks like when no one is watching. They guide you through the moments that build confidence—the kind that doesn't shake when life does. And they'll teach you how to step into the identity of the woman you say you're becoming, not someday when everything is perfect, but now, as you are.

> *The truth is simple and wild and a little terrifying: You don't become her first. You decide to be her first. And then you build a life that reflects that decision.*

Welcome to the part of the journey where everything you've learned starts to take shape. Welcome to the part where you meet yourself again—this time with open eyes and both feet on the ground. *Welcome to becoming her now.*

Chapter 4

Healing Isn't a Prerequisite—It's a Process

The morning after that kitchen moment felt strangely quiet. Not peaceful quiet—more like the air right after a storm, when everything is still, but nothing is the same. I had drawn a line in the sand the night before. I wasn't going to shrink my way through my own life anymore. I meant it. I felt it. But once the adrenaline faded, something else crept in. The real question wasn't whether I wanted a different life. It was whether I knew how to live one.

That's the part no one tells you about your "enough is enough" moment. The declaration feels powerful, cinematic even, but the next morning is honest in a way that can knock the wind out of you. Because once the dust settles, you're left with the truth: deciding to change is one thing. Learning how to hold yourself through that change is another. I woke up realizing I didn't just need a new identity, I needed support. I needed someone who wasn't tangled in my habits, my history, or my patterns to help me find my way back to myself.

There was a quiet knowing that if I kept trying to do this alone, I'd end up right back where I started. I had spent years convincing myself that getting help meant something was wrong with me, that I should be able to figure it out on my own. But choosing support before everything was on fire? That was new. That was growth. That was the beginning of leading myself instead of abandoning myself.

I booked the appointment. It wasn't about courage. I was just tired of acting like I didn't need the help. And that's how this chapter begins—not with a dramatic collapse, but with a woman sitting in her car on a Thursday morning, staring at a beige therapy building she almost talked herself out of walking into. A woman who was starting to realize that healing isn't a destination you arrive at once you've earned it. It's a process you choose while you're still in the mess, still unsure, still becoming.

This is when I walked into support before I felt ready. When I stopped performing "fine" and started telling the truth. When healing stopped being an end goal and started becoming something I lived inside of—imperfectly, honestly, and in real time.

The Day I Finally Asked for Help

I ended up in therapy at a time when my life looked fine on the outside. The babies were healthy. My relationship was good. The house was full, and every night I went to bed telling myself I should feel grateful. But something still felt off. I couldn't explain it. Nothing was wrong, but I didn't feel fully in my own life. And the more I tried to push past it and just keep going, the heavier it got.

The morning I finally went to the appointment my hands were shaking so badly I wrote my name, birthdate, and phone number wrong on the intake form. I wasn't ashamed of needing help. I was ashamed that I needed it when nothing was technically wrong. I kept thinking, other women have it so much harder. The girl I was three years ago needed this. Who am I to need support now? Who am I to say I'm struggling when my life looks this good on paper? That guilt kept me quiet for months. That guilt almost kept me from going.

The day of the appointment, I dropped the kids off with their Nana and drove to the office with my stomach in knots. My mind kept trying to talk me out of it. You're fine. You're being dramatic. Just go home and have a shower—you'll feel better. I even put my blinker on to turn around once. But something in me—a small, tired part I had been ignoring for way too long—whispered, not this time. Keep going.

The building wasn't anything special. Beige walls, scuffed floors, a smell that reminded me of old carpet and peppermint tea bags. I sat in the car for a few minutes before going in, gripping the steering wheel so hard my fingers went numb. It wasn't fear of the therapist. It was fear of what I might say out loud. Fear that if I told the truth, I wouldn't be able to stuff it back down again.

When I finally walked inside, the receptionist smiled at me like I wasn't unraveling on the spot. She handed me a clipboard with the intake form, and I swear my brain went blank. Occupation. I stared at the empty line for a long time.

I wrote "stay-at-home mother," and felt that quiet discomfort rise, the kind that makes you question if what you are is enough, even when you know it should be.

Then came the question I'll never forget: "What brings you in today?"

I didn't know how to answer that, so I wrote the truest thing I could manage: "I guess I just don't really know who I am anymore or who I am supposed to be."

When the therapist finally called my name, she had the kind of presence that made me want to both cry and run away. Soft eyes, warm voice, calm energy and perfectly polished. The office was exactly what you'd expect: muted colors, a bookshelf of titles I pretended not to read, a couch that looked like it had heard centuries of secrets. I sat down, crossed my legs, uncrossed them, crossed them again. She smiled gently and asked where I wanted to start.

I opened my mouth, but no words came out at first. When they finally did, they weren't polished or organized or thoughtful.

They were messy. They were rushed. They were everything I'd been carrying but hadn't said out loud in years . . . or ever. I told her about the kids, about the exhaustion, about the mornings I felt like I was watching someone else live my life. I told her about the pressure to be grateful when my gratitude and grief were tangled together in knots I couldn't separate. I told her about the woman I thought I was becoming and the woman I felt like inside—and how the gap between them scared me.

She nodded, listened, waited. And then she asked the question that cracked me open.

"When did you learn that you had to earn your right to rest?"

I don't know why that question did it. Maybe because no one had ever asked me something so direct. Maybe because it named something I didn't know I was allowed to name. Or maybe because deep down, I already knew the answer. I flashed instantly to my teenage years, to the girl who felt like she had to prove her worth just to exist. The girl who lost her mom and quietly decided she needed to be low-maintenance, grateful, never a burden. The girl who believed love was something you earned by staying small, staying quiet, staying easy.

It was the first time it hit me that I had been living my adult life through that old script. I wasn't tired because motherhood was hard. I was tired because I didn't know how to let myself be a human being with needs. I wasn't overwhelmed because my life was chaotic. I was overwhelmed because I was still performing the version of me who believed she had to earn her place in it.

I remember looking down at my hands in my lap, embarrassed by how obvious it suddenly felt. She didn't say it with judgment. She said it with compassion. But compassion can sting when you're not used to receiving it. I felt like someone had found the loose thread in my entire identity and gently tugged.

We spent the rest of the session unraveling that thread. I told her about the pressure I put on myself to be "fine." About how I minimized my feelings because other people had it worse (and I *knew* worse). About the guilt I felt for struggling when my life looked good. I told her about the morning in the kitchen—the slump, the burnout, the moment I caught myself disappearing. She didn't flinch or rush to fix me. She simply sat there, holding space for the truth I had been too afraid to claim.

Somewhere near the end of the session, she said something that still echoes in my bones: "You're not wrong for feeling this. You're exhausted from trying to be the version of you everyone else needed."

And for the first time in years, I exhaled. A long, shaky, chest-heavy exhale that felt like it came from the girl I used to be. I didn't cry. Not then. The tears would come later, in the car, in the shower, in the grocery store aisle when a random song made my throat tighten. But in that moment, I felt something loosen inside me. Something soften. Something open.

She asked me if I'd like to come back the following week. Old me would've said, "I'll think about it." But the woman sitting on that couch—the one who had just admitted out loud that she didn't know who she was—knew she needed to say yes. I was finally ready to stop pretending.

When the session ended, I walked to my car feeling both raw and relieved. I sat in the driver's seat, stared out the windshield, and whispered to myself, "Okay. We're doing this." Not the performance. Not the pretending. The real work. The kind where you don't wait until everything is burning to ask for help. The kind where you choose support because you're worth supporting.

I didn't magically become healed after that day. I didn't suddenly wake up knowing who I was. But something shifted. I had taken the first step out of survival mode and into something gentler, something more honest, something that felt like the beginning of coming home to myself.

And that's what this chapter is really about—the moment you stop waiting to be worthy of help. The moment you walk into a beige office and tell the truth before you're ready. The moment you stop performing "fine" and start choosing something real.

This was the day I stopped trying to earn my right to exist. This was the moment I admitted I wanted more for myself. This was the beginning of learning that healing isn't something you finish before you start living. Healing is what happens when you choose to live.

The Lie of Being Fully Healed

No one warns you about the fantasy you build about healing. The fantasy that tells you there will be a day—an exact day—when everything locks into place. When the past stops stinging, when your nervous system stops flaring, when you stop second-guessing every decision you make. A day when you finally "arrive." I believed in that day more than I believed in myself. And for years, that belief kept me stuck.

It showed up subtly at first. I'd say things like "I just need to heal a little more," or "Once I deal with this, then I'll feel ready." Underneath it was the same old story in a prettier outfit. I was still waiting to feel like a woman who deserved the life she wanted. I was still waiting for someone—anyone—to tell me that I'd done enough inner work to finally begin. I didn't realize it at the time, but what I was calling healing was actually hiding. Hiding inside reflection. Hiding inside "working on myself." Convincing myself I needed more clarity, more understanding, more time, before I was allowed to actually move.

But healing doesn't work like that. It doesn't give you the satisfaction of a certificate, or a finish line, or a clear moment where someone stamps your forehead and says, "Congratulations, you are now fully healed. You may proceed with living." If anything, it moves with you. It evolves as you evolve. It shifts as life shifts around you. Healing isn't something you finish so you can start your life. It's something that happens inside your life.

Sitting in that beige office, feet tucked under the chair, hands clenched in my lap, it hit me in the slowest, quietest way. I wasn't here because I had fallen apart. I was here because I was finally telling the truth: I didn't know who I was anymore. I had been performing competence, performing gratitude, performing strength for so long that I had forgotten the part where I got to be human. I walked into therapy because I couldn't keep pretending that I was okay. And that's the part no one talks about. You can look functional on the outside and still be unraveling in the privacy of your own mind. You can have a partner who loves you, babies who cling to you, a life that looks stable—and still feel like something inside you is unfinished. Not wrong. Not damaged. Just . . . unsorted. Unnamed. Unclaimed.

That was my problem. I kept thinking healing meant fixing myself. I kept thinking it meant erasing every old wound and every old insecurity until nothing hurt anymore. Until I never flinched. Until I never spiraled. Until I never felt fragile or uncertain. I thought healing was about becoming unbreakable. I didn't understand yet that it was about learning how to bend without abandoning myself.

My therapist listened to me spill everything: my confusion, my exhaustion, the way I kept waiting for the "healed version" of me to show up and save the day. She didn't rush. She didn't nod in that over-sympathetic way that makes you feel like a charity case. She just waited until I ran out of words. Then she asked, "Where did you learn that you have to be fully healed before you're allowed to live your life?"

I didn't know how to answer. Because the truth was, I didn't learn it from one moment. I learned it from everywhere. From a culture obsessed with glow-up timelines. From friends who whispered about working on themselves but were really just stalling for the perfect conditions to appear. From my own fear masquerading as responsibility. But mostly, I learned it from the part of me that still believed love, rest, confidence—everything good—had to be earned.

Healing became the new ladder. The new measuring stick. The new way to prove I was worthy.

But in that office, something clicked for the first time. The way I had been seeing myself . . . it wasn't even true. I was just human.

A woman who had lived through a lot, who had navigated life without a map for so long that she forgot she was allowed to reach for support before the emergency alarms went off.

I kept thinking healing would erase the ache. Instead, it asked me to feel it. To stop outrunning it. To sit with the parts of myself I had managed in silence for too many years. And the moment I let myself do that, even clumsily, something shifted. I stopped fighting what I was feeling. I stopped trying to fix it. I just let it be there. Healing wasn't a destination. It was an orientation. A posture. A way of being in relationship with myself.

I had imagined healing as a grand reveal. A before-and-after moment. A version of me who walked into every room glowing with certainty. What I got was far quieter. Healing showed up in the way I started telling the truth faster. In the way I stopped apologizing for needing rest. In the way I no longer spiraled for days over one intrusive thought. In the way I could say, "I'm struggling," without feeling like I was failing.

Healing didn't make my triggers disappear. It made them less powerful. It made me less afraid of myself.

And that's when I learned the part that changed everything: you don't become *her* by finishing your healing. You become *her* by living while you heal. By choosing movement over perfection. By showing up in the mess, not after it's cleaned.

That's why this part matters so much. Because so many women are doing what I did—waiting to feel complete before they begin. But healing is built in motion. You don't get clarity and then act; you act your way into clarity. You don't get confidence and then show up; you show up until confidence starts to feel like home. You don't become *her* and then live; you live like her until your identity catches up.

> *If you're waiting until you feel perfectly healed, your life will stay on pause forever. Because the work doesn't hand you permission. You give it to yourself.*

That day in therapy was the moment I stopped treating healing as a prerequisite and started treating it as a companion. The moment

I realized I didn't need to be flawless to grow, to lead myself, to step into the woman I wanted to become. I just needed to be willing.

I didn't walk out of that office fixed. I didn't walk out with a laminated identity or a new personality. I walked out with something better: permission to be in process. Permission to show up anyway. Permission to write my next chapter without waiting for my old wounds to disappear first.

Healing wasn't a finish line. It was a doorway. And stepping through it, shaky and unsure, was the first real act of self-trust I had ever made.

Healing in Motion

Healing felt like tiny shifts that barely made sense at first. It felt like catching myself one breath sooner. One spiral sooner. One self-abandonment sooner. It felt like realizing that healing wasn't the work I did after life calmed down—it was the work happening inside the chaos.

For years, I thought growth meant never being triggered again. I thought healing meant the old patterns disappearing completely, like wiping a hard drive clean. But when I finally let myself be honest, I saw something softer, truer: healing wasn't about eliminating my old reactions. It was about meeting them differently. It was about noticing where I would normally shrink—and choosing not to. It was about recognizing the moment my nervous system slipped into old roles and deciding, gently but firmly, "We're not doing that anymore."

This is where healing lives: in the tiny gap between the woman you've been and the woman you're becoming. That gap used to swallow me whole. I'd fall into it for days, convinced I'd regressed, convinced I'd failed. Now, that gap became the place where I practiced. Where I rewired. Where I chose to stay with myself long enough to change the ending.

Healing in motion looked nothing like the polished idea I had built in my head. It looked like apologizing sooner instead of stewing in shame for days. It looked like noticing my resentment rising and naming the need underneath it instead of exploding. It looked like feeling anxiety spike in my chest and taking a breath instead of running from it. It looked like the smallest shifts—ones no one else would ever see—but each shift was a quiet revolution.

And the wildest part? It wasn't about perfection. It wasn't even about consistency. It was about honesty. It was about letting myself admit that I was still learning how to trust myself. That I was rebuilding something I never had words for. That I wasn't doing it wrong—I was simply doing it consciously.

What no one prepares you for is that healing, when it's working, can feel anticlimactic. You expect fireworks, and instead you get something quieter. A shift in how you respond. A moment where you don't go as far as you used to. Where things move through you differently. And over time, those small changes start to add up. You realize you're not stuck in the same patterns. You're not carrying things as long. You're not reacting the way you once did. That's when it hits you: the way you're living your life has changed.

I remember one afternoon when I was wiping down the counter after an exhausting morning. My son had spilled cereal everywhere, my daughter was cranky, and my patience was paper thin. Old me would have snapped, then spiraled in guilt for hours. But that day, I caught the impulse. I stopped. I took a breath so shaky it barely qualified as a breath. And I said out loud, "You're safe. You're doing your best." Nobody heard it but me—yet it changed everything. It interrupted the spiral. It softened the edge. That's healing in motion: the private moments where you choose compassion instead of self-punishment.

I used to believe that awareness was the entire point. That noticing my patterns meant I was "awake enough." But awareness without self-trust is just watching yourself live the same life over and over again. Healing needed something deeper than awareness. It needed action. It needed me to respond differently, even when the old response felt easier. Especially when it felt easier.

I started to see healing the same way I saw learning to walk again after an injury—shaky, awkward, humbling. You don't beat yourself up for limping. You don't shame yourself for wobbling. You celebrate the step. You celebrate the attempt. You celebrate the courage to put weight on something that once hurt you. That's what healing felt like. Every time I chose a new response, I was putting weight on a part of my identity I hadn't trusted before. I was proving it could hold me.

And slowly—almost unnoticeably—those choices started adding up. They started building a new baseline. A new sense of what was normal for me. A new relationship with myself that didn't disappear the moment life got loud.

Healing also revealed the truth about who I was when things weren't going well. I had always assumed healing meant that I would eventually "transcend" difficult seasons. But the more I lived inside this work, the more I realized the point wasn't to avoid the hard—it was to meet it with different energy. A more grounded energy. A more self-led energy. A more compassionate energy. That shift alone changed the texture of my life.

There were days when healing meant crying on the kitchen floor, letting myself feel what I had pushed down for years. There were days when healing looked like texting my husband and saying, "I need 10 minutes alone," instead of powering through resentment. There were days when healing looked like saying no to plans I would have caved to six months earlier. And there were days when healing looked like doing absolutely nothing except noticing the urge to abandon myself—and choosing not to.

When I think back to that season now, it wasn't clean or easy to explain. It was messy. Some days felt like progress, some days didn't. I was just figuring it out as I went, learning how to be in my life without constantly waiting for something to go wrong. Catching the moments where I would've spiraled and choosing something different instead. And slowly, I started giving myself a chance, even before I felt fully ready. That's the part I want you to feel in your bones: healing happens while you're living. Not before it. Not after it. In it.

It happens when you're tired. When your kids are screaming. When you're overwhelmed. When your life feels too full or not full enough. Healing isn't waiting for you on the other side of a perfect moment. It's happening the moment you decide to meet yourself with honesty and stay with yourself long enough to move differently.

The real proof of healing is subtle. It's in the way you catch that old voice and gently redirect it. It's in the way you speak to yourself when no one hears. It's in the choices you make when no one will ever know. It's in the way you stop abandoning yourself the second fear shows up. It's in the way the old story still whispers, but no longer runs the show.

This Is Where You Begin Again

When I think about the girl I was at 15, I don't think she ever imagined this version of me.

She didn't imagine sitting in a therapist's office, saying things out loud she didn't even have words for back then. She didn't imagine learning how to stay with herself instead of shutting down. She didn't imagine that healing wouldn't come in one big moment, but in a hundred small ones she would have to choose over and over again.

If I could sit with her now, I wouldn't try to explain everything. I wouldn't tell her it all works out. I wouldn't tell her she becomes strong. I wouldn't hand her some polished version of what's ahead. I would just sit beside her and say, you don't have to keep leaving yourself to get through this.

Because that is what I spent years doing. Leaving in the quiet ways. Leaving in the moments no one else could see. Leaving every time something felt too heavy, too uncomfortable, too much to face all at once. I learned how to move on quickly, how to push things down, how to keep functioning. From the outside, it looked like I was holding everything together, but inside, I was slowly disconnecting from myself.

Healing was the first time I stopped doing that. The first time I stayed long enough to feel what was actually there. The first time I let things be messy without rushing to clean them up. The first time I stopped trying to manage everything and just told the truth, even when I didn't fully understand it yet.

There was no moment where everything suddenly made sense. No version of me that arrived fully healed and untouched by what I had been through. It was slower than that. Quieter than that. It looked like showing up to sessions I didn't always want to be in. Sitting with thoughts I used to avoid. Noticing the urge to shut down and choosing to stay a few seconds longer.

Over time, those seconds added up. Not into perfection, and not into certainty, but into something steadier. Something more honest. A version of me who didn't run at the first sign of discomfort. A version of me who could stay present in her own life without constantly bracing for what might happen next.

Healing didn't give me a finished version of myself. It gave me a way back. Back to my voice, back to my needs, back to the parts of me I had learned to ignore just to get through.

But coming back to yourself is only the beginning.

There is a difference between hearing yourself and trusting yourself. A difference between knowing what you need and actually choosing it. A difference between recognizing your patterns and responding differently when they show up again.

That is where things start to change. That is where your life begins to move in a new direction. Not in theory, not in reflection, but in real time, in the moments when you decide whether to follow what is familiar or choose what is true.

That is the part no one can do for you.

And that is where we are going next.

Because knowing yourself matters. Trusting yourself is what changes your life.

Key Points

Before you move on, take a second and sit with this:

- You don't have to be fully healed before you're allowed to live your life.
- Healing lives in the tiny gap between the woman you've been and the woman you're becoming.
- Awareness can only take you so far; unless you trust yourself to move differently, you'll keep living the same loop.

Chapter 5

Building Self-Trust

It wasn't about productivity. Or hustle. Or being that girl. Setting my alarm for 5 a.m. had nothing to do with proving anything to the world. It was a promise I made to myself. A quiet, personal decision.

Because when I wake up at 5, I get something I don't get any other time of day: me. Just me. No one climbing on me. No breakfast requests. No toys clattering to the floor. No chaos spilling into my thoughts before I've even had a sip of coffee. Just an hour of stillness where I can breathe, stretch, taste my coffee while it's actually hot, and remember who I am outside of the noise.

It wasn't about curating the perfect, Instagram-worthy morning routine. It was about alignment. It was about proving to myself that my needs were worth honoring—even when no one was watching.

When I first became a mom, I completely lost myself in the blur of diapers and feedings and exhaustion. There were days I'd look in the mirror and not recognize the woman staring back. I loved my babies more than anything, but somewhere in the middle of keeping everyone else alive, I'd stopped checking in on me.

The woman with dreams, ideas, a voice. I remember one morning sitting on the rocking chair in my son's room, after he was finally asleep on my chest, scrolling social media and seeing women who looked like they had time and energy and purpose—and I thought, *When do I get to feel like that?*

That question stayed with me for months. I'd tuck it away between loads of laundry, telling myself I'd figure it out later. But "later" never came. Until one night, after another long day that felt exactly like the one before, I put the kids to bed, walked into the kitchen, and thought, *I can't keep doing this on autopilot.* I needed one hour. Just one. So I set the alarm.

I laid out my robe and slippers. Put my candle and lighter on the counter so they'd be ready. I even poured water into the kettle the night before so I'd have one less excuse in the morning. I was stacking the deck in my own favor—making it impossible to talk myself out of it when the moment came.

And still, when 5 a.m. came? I wanted to cry. The room was dark in that way only early-morning darkness is—not the soft glow of evening, but the deep, heavy kind that makes your eyelids want to stay shut. The air was cool enough to make my warm bed feel like the safest place in the world. My blanket had molded perfectly to me, like it was saying, *Don't go. Just stay here.*

My body felt like it was made of bricks. Every muscle begged me to roll over. I could already hear the faint creak of floorboards in the hallway—one of the kids stirring—and instantly my brain jumped in: *well, that's it. They're going to be up any minute. What's the point of getting up now if the peace is going to be broken?*

And then the other voice. The familiar one. The one I knew too well. *Just sleep. You can try again tomorrow. This doesn't really matter.*

It's wild how quickly you can start bargaining with yourself when comfort is involved. In that moment, I had a whole conversation in my head: *you're tired. You've had a long week. You deserve the rest. Missing one day won't hurt. It's not like anyone's going to know.*

And that last thought . . . *No one will know.*

That's when it hit me: *I will know.*

I thought about all the other times I'd told myself I'd do something and then didn't. All the tiny promises I'd abandoned, thinking they were too small to matter. All the times I'd let myself down without realizing the weight it was adding to my life. Then I remembered something I'd scribbled in my journal weeks earlier: *I feel most like* her *when I keep my word to myself.*

That version of me? She doesn't cancel on her peace. She doesn't snooze her alignment. She doesn't wait for perfect conditions to honor what matters.

So I peeled the covers back before I could change my mind. The shock of the cold air on my skin made me flinch, but I stood up anyway. Slipped on my robe and shuffled into the kitchen, the quiet slap of my slippers on the tile echoing in the stillness. The kettle was already sitting there, water filled—which was the past me, looking out for current me. *Thanks, girl.* I pressed the button, and the soft hum of it heating filled the silence. Lit the candle and watched the little flame catch, dancing against the dark.

I leaned on the counter for a moment, eyes half-closed, listening to the tiny pops from the wick and the gentle hiss of the water heating. It wasn't inspiring on the surface. But it was mine.

That first morning, I didn't know what to do with the quiet. I sat there, staring into my mug, trying not to open my phone, and I felt awkwardly aware of the silence.

But as the days went on, that silence stopped feeling uncomfortable. It became the place where my thoughts got clearer, where ideas started coming back, where I could finally hear myself again. It's where I began reconnecting with my voice—the one that had been buried under everything I had been carrying for so long.

Some mornings I journaled. Some mornings I cried. Some mornings I sat there doing absolutely nothing except reminding myself that I existed outside of who I was to everyone else. That hour was my rebellion. My reminder that I mattered, even when the world didn't need me yet.

Did I feel wildly accomplished? Not really. But I felt present. I felt proud. Because that moment—me, in the dark, showing up for myself with no audience, no applause, no checklist to cross off—that was her.

That was the real expansion. It's not loud. It's not shiny. It's not something the world claps for or even notices. But it's the moment you take your identity back. The moment you say to yourself, *I matter. My needs matter. My peace matters.* And you don't need to justify it to anyone.

That's the kind of moment that changes everything. It's not about how big the action looks, it's about the fact that you followed through. You didn't push it off or tell yourself you'd deal with it later. You moved when you said you would, and in doing that, you started operating as the woman who trusts herself to follow through. Even if your eyes are barely open. Even if your kids are already awake. Even if no one sees it but you.

And that? That is what creates the life you keep saying you want. One decision at a time. One quiet morning at a time. One vote for her—over and over again.

Why Self-Trust Is the Backbone of Becoming *Her*

Self-trust is built in the moments no one sees. It's built when you follow through on what you said you would do. When you make a decision and stand in it. When you stop outsourcing your next move and start backing your own voice. It's quiet, but it's decisive. And over time, it becomes the difference between knowing what you want and actually living it. Self-trust is the part that lives underneath all of that. It's the part you meet at 5 a.m., in the dark, when no one is watching and no one is cheering and no one will ever know whether you got out of bed or hit snooze. It's the part that determines who you actually become, not who you intend to become.

Every woman thinks she needs confidence. Every woman thinks she needs motivation. Every woman thinks she needs discipline, strategy, clarity, and a perfectly organized three-step plan. But the truth is without self-trust, none of it sticks. Motivation fades.

Confidence wobbles. Discipline cracks. Plans change. But the relationship you have with yourself—whether you believe your own word or not—decides everything.

I didn't understand this for a long time. I used to think confidence was the feeling you got *after* you had evidence. I used to think you needed to see progress before you could believe in yourself. I used to think you needed to "feel ready" before you could take the first step. But standing in my kitchen, robe wrapped tight, tea steaming, the world still asleep—that's when I realized it was backwards. You don't become confident and then take action. You take action and then you build confidence. You earn self-trust by showing yourself who you are, not by waiting for the feeling to show up first.

Most women don't have a confidence problem. They have a credibility problem—with themselves. They don't trust that they'll follow through, because they have years of proof that they won't. It's not a lack of desire or discipline. It's the pattern of leaving themselves in the moments that matter. When things feel overwhelming, when fear gets louder, when comfort pulls harder, they step away from what they actually want without even realizing it. And when you abandon yourself enough times, your nervous system learns one thing: we don't do what we say we'll do.

That's the real reason you shrink. That's the real reason you hesitate. That's the real reason you feel stuck: because deep down, you don't yet believe yourself. You don't believe your word. And if you can't trust yourself, how can you ever expect yourself to take the risks, hold the boundaries, say the no, claim the yes, or stretch into the version of you you've been dreaming about?

It's not the goal that's the problem. It's the identity behind the goal.

Self-trust is identity work. It is the foundation underneath every choice you make. It is the quiet agreement between you and the woman you are becoming. It is the invisible thread that connects your present self to your future self. If that thread is frayed, everything feels unstable. But when that thread is strong—when you trust yourself deeply—you stop bargaining with your potential. You stop negotiating with your excuses. You stop waiting for permission to move.

Imagine this: two women standing in front of the same opportunity. Same resources. Same circumstances. Same potential. One steps forward. One steps back. What separates them isn't talent. It isn't intelligence. It isn't luck. It isn't time. It isn't confidence. It's self-trust. One woman believes she will show up for herself, even when it gets uncomfortable. The other believes she'll crumble the moment it does. One believes she'll hold herself steady. The other believes she'll disappear. One believes she can rely on her future self. The other doesn't even know who her future self is.

Self-trust is the bridge between knowing and becoming. It's the missing piece between *I want to change* and *I changed.* Every decision you make—every micro-choice, every small follow-through, every moment you choose you—becomes a brick in the foundation of your identity. You don't just build habits. You build a woman you can count on.

And the woman who trusts herself is unstoppable. She doesn't move from panic. She doesn't move from pressure. She doesn't move from comparison. She moves from intention. She moves from clarity. She moves from integrity. She moves because she said she would.

Think about how many times you've abandoned yourself in tiny, almost invisible ways. The workout you promised yourself. The project you said you'd start. The boundary you swore you'd hold. The routine you vowed to commit to. The bedtime you told yourself was nonnegotiable. The promise to rest. The promise to speak up. The promise to try. The promise to stop waiting for perfect.

Every time you whispered "later," every time you said, "next time," every time you said, "it doesn't matter," you weren't just skipping the thing—you were voting against your identity. You were casting a ballot for the version of you that hides, hesitates, delays, and doubts. You were strengthening the old story instead of choosing the new one.

Self-trust flips that script. It says, *I don't shrink back into who I used to be. I choose the woman I'm becoming. I choose* her *with my actions, not just my intentions.*

And here's the wildest part: the moment you start keeping promises to yourself—even tiny ones, even boring ones, even ones no one else would ever know about—your energy shifts. Your posture shifts. Your voice shifts. Your relationships shift. Your decisions shift. Your entire life shifts, because you are no longer negotiating with your own word. You are no longer living in the tension between what you want and what you believe you're capable of.

> *When you trust yourself, you become a woman with direction. A woman with a plan. A woman with a spine. A woman who knows she can rely on herself in the moments that matter most.*

Self-trust is not the radiant part of transformation; it is the part that decides the trajectory of your entire life. It determines the goals you set, the risks you take, the boundaries you hold, the opportunities you say yes to, the relationships you choose, the habits you build, the stories you release, and the identity you live from. It is the source of confidence, not the by-product.

Confidence doesn't build self-trust. Self-trust builds confidence.

And once you get that—once you understand that the woman you want to be is built in the unseen, uncelebrated moments of your life—you stop waiting for transformation to feel dramatic. You stop waiting for proof. You realize the most life-changing decisions you ever make won't happen in front of a crowd. They'll happen in the dark, at 5 a.m., when no one is watching but you . . . and the woman you are becoming.

How to Build Self-Trust Without Overwhelming Your Nervous System

There's something we don't talk about enough when it comes to self-trust: your body always arrives to the moment before your mind does. You can decide you're going to wake up at 5 a.m. or speak up in the meeting or post the thing that scares you, but when you go to do it, your nervous system has opinions. Sometimes loud ones. The heart racing. The throat tightening. The urge to run, hide, or collapse into the old familiar patterns. And for years I made the mistake of thinking those sensations meant I was weak, uncommitted, or not cut out for the life I wanted. I thought, "If this was truly meant for me, I wouldn't feel like this." But that couldn't be further from the truth. The only reason your nervous system activates is because it's trying to protect you. It learned—usually very early—what feels safe and what feels threatening. And here's the plot twist: even the things you want can feel threatening if they're unfamiliar. Which means the real work of self-trust isn't forcing your way through the discomfort. It's learning how to create safety while you stretch into a new identity.

Your nervous system isn't the enemy of your growth. It's the gatekeeper of your capacity. When you're used to abandoning yourself, dimming your wants, or doing everything in your power not to be seen, even a tiny self-honoring action can register as danger. The text you send, the boundary you set, the early morning alarm you honor—your body doesn't evaluate it based on whether it's "good for you." It evaluates it based on whether you've survived it before. This is why so many women say, "I know what to do, but I can't make myself do it." It's not a mindset problem. It's a safety problem.

So if you've ever felt frustrated that you can't push yourself harder or faster, I want you to hear this: self-trust isn't built by shocking your system into compliance. It's built through micro-safe steps that gently expand your capacity. The same way you wouldn't walk into a gym after a year away and try to deadlift your bodyweight, you don't build identity by demanding your nervous system jump from zero to full visibility overnight. When you force yourself into extremes, your body doesn't say, *Wow, she's committed.* It says, *We're not safe*, and shuts you down. That shutdown isn't failure—it's protection. But when we don't understand this, we shame ourselves for something our body was literally designed to do.

This is why self-trust and nervous system safety are inseparable. Every time you follow through on a small promise in a way that feels tolerable—not traumatizing—you teach your body that you won't abandon it. You teach it that change is safe. You teach it that you're leading now, not the old fear patterns that used to call the shots. When your body feels safe with you, everything else becomes easier. Decisions land cleaner. Action feels less dramatic. Confidence grows in the background while you live your life. And you start to realize self-trust isn't a push. It's a conversation. It's you saying to your body, *I won't drag you somewhere you're not ready to go, but I also won't let you keep me small.* That balance is where the magic lives.

One of the biggest shifts in my own life came when I started asking myself a new question: *What is one step forward that my nervous system can handle today?* Not the fantasy step. Not the dramatic leap. Not the thing I would do if I weren't scared. The real step. The one that stretched me just enough to build trust, but not enough to knock me back into shutdown. Some days that step was waking up at 5 a.m. Other days it was getting out of bed at all. Some days it was going somewhere new in public with my kids when I didn't know the parking situation (if you know you know). Other days it was just being more honest with my boundaries. Self-trust doesn't grow from the size of the step but from the consistency of it. The repetition is what rewires you.

The more I practiced this, the more I noticed something subtle but life-changing: the line between "unsafe" and "unfamiliar" started to move. Things that once sent me straight into freeze didn't overload me anymore. My nervous system had evidence that I could hold myself. That I wouldn't abandon the moment things felt uncomfortable. That my word meant something. And that's when I realized the truth every woman needs: *your nervous system isn't keeping you small. It's waiting for you to lead.*

This is what nervous system regulation looks like inside the self-trust journey. It's not about deep breathing your way through panic or trying to "Zen" your way into big decisions. It's about creating conditions that make it possible for your body to stay online while you expand. It's putting your phone in the kitchen at night because your body can't settle when it's buzzing beside your pillow. It's saying no to one more commitment because overwhelm isn't a personality trait—it's a capacity mismatch. It's choosing five minutes of journaling instead of an hour because your nervous system needs a win, not another expectation to fail. It's giving yourself a softer morning when the night before gutted you emotionally. Regulation is not retreat. It's resourcing.

And when you start living this way—when you stop bulldozing your body and start partnering with it—you unlock a new level of power. That's when self-trust becomes sustainable. You start following through because you want to, not because you're white-knuckling your way through pressure. You start stretching yourself because you know you can hold the discomfort, not because you're trying to outrun it. You begin making decisions from an anchored place rather than a reactive one. And that steadiness is what makes your identity shift stick. Anyone can force a habit for a week. But a woman who knows how to regulate herself through expansion? She's unstoppable.

And here's the part I want you to really take in: sometimes the bravest thing you can do is slow the pace, not speed it up. Sometimes the most self-trusting move is choosing the step that builds capacity instead of the one that impresses people. Sometimes the most expansive moment is the one when you pause, breathe, and remind your body that it's safe now. That's not weakness. That's leadership. That's you stepping into *her* identity in real time—not by pushing past yourself, but by standing with yourself.

> *Building self-trust isn't about bypassing your body. It's about rewiring your relationship with it. Your nervous system doesn't need you to be fearless. It needs you to be honest.*

Your nervous system needs you to move at the speed of safety, not the speed of pressure. It needs you to listen when something is too much, and lead when something is just unfamiliar. The more you do that, the more your inner world syncs with the identity you're choosing. And then suddenly the things that used to terrify you become things you do on a random Tuesday without even thinking.

Same moments. Different version of you. You don't force yourself into the woman you want to be. You start showing up as her in small, real ways, teaching your nervous system it's safe to hold that version of you, until it no longer feels like a stretch. It just feels like who you are.

Rewriting the Self-Trust Narrative

Most women don't realize they're living inside a story they didn't write. A story inherited from childhood, from patterns they watched, from the versions of themselves they had to become to survive seasons that asked too much of them. A story that says, *I always quit*, or *I never follow through*, or *I can't trust myself to keep promises*. A story that feels like truth, but is just repetition with a convincing costume. Every time you break your word to yourself, the old narrative gets louder. Every time you say you'll start tomorrow, every time you shrink instead of speaking up, every time you numb out instead of tuning in, your brain files it as evidence: See? This is who we are. And because identity is built through repetition, the story becomes familiar. And because familiar feels safe, even when it hurts, you stay loyal to it. Not on purpose—your nervous system simply clings to the version of you it already knows how to be. But here's the part we never learn: *identity stories can be rewritten*. They're not final drafts. They're patterns. And patterns only hold power as long as you keep rehearsing them.

Rewriting your self-trust narrative is not about pretending you're a brand-new woman who has no history. It's about interrupting the automatic script that says you can't count on yourself and creating enough micro-evidence to prove that's no longer true. Most women try to do this with a dramatic overhaul—new routines, new habits, new outfits—thinking if they change everything at once, the old identity won't catch up. But the old identity always catches up because you haven't built the evidence yet that you do what you say you will do. That is the real work of self-trust. It isn't curated or loud or Instagrammable. It's private. It's built in the dark. It's built in the moments no one else sees.

Stop Waiting to Get It Perfect

One of the most important shifts in rewriting your self-trust story is letting go of the idea that you have to become perfect to be trustworthy. Perfection is a trap designed to keep you from beginning. You don't need to flawlessly execute every promise to build self-trust; you just need to start keeping one more promise today than you kept yesterday. Your self-trust story begins shifting the moment you decide to make your commitments smaller, cleaner, more honest, and rooted in who you actually are right now, not who you'll be once you finally get your life together. If the old you promised herself impossible standards and then beat herself up for failing, the new you chooses promises so aligned that following through feels like relief, not punishment. That's how you start rewriting the story: you make your word easier to believe.

A powerful way to begin is to notice the voice of the old script without judging it. Noticing is awareness, but noticing with compassion is transformation. Instead of *Why can't I stick to anything?* you shift into *Oh, this is the part where I usually abandon myself.* That one shift turns shame into choice. And choice is where self-trust is rebuilt. When you catch the old pattern with tenderness instead of self-criticism, you create space to choose the micro-move that leads you toward *her* instead of back into the version you've outgrown. Rewrite requires softness, not pressure. It requires honesty, not perfection. It requires the willingness to meet yourself where you are, instead of where you think you "should" be by now.

Build Proof

Then comes the second layer: creating proof. Not chasing it, not performing it, not broadcasting it—creating it quietly, consistently, until you begin to believe the new story you're writing. Proof is built through repetition, the same way the old identity was. If you want to become a woman who trusts herself, you have to show yourself your own reliability again and again. This is why micro-promises matter so much. A 10-minute walk. A single paragraph written. One honest conversation. Drinking a glass of water before your coffee. Setting your phone in another room for the first 10 minutes of your morning. These tiny acts are not insignificant; they are blueprints. They are signals to your nervous system: this is who we are now. This is what we do. And once your nervous system feels the steadiness of your actions, self-trust becomes less of a concept and more of a lived experience.

Avoid Performance

Another piece of rewriting your narrative is breaking the cycle of performative self-trust. That's when you follow through only if someone is watching, only if there's validation, only if it earns approval. The old you performed. The new you practices. Performing drains self-trust because it treats your integrity like a stage instead of a relationship. Practicing builds self-trust because it honors your integrity even when no one else will ever know what you did. The most magnetic women are not the ones who look consistent on the outside—they're the ones who are consistent when it's invisible. That's why the thought *No one will know, but I will* is so powerful. It's not about proving anything outwardly; it's about becoming someone you can rely on inwardly. That shift is what changes everything.

Stop Waiting for Monday

Breaking the start-over loop is another essential part of rewriting your story. The old identity loves dramatic restarts: Monday morning, new month, new year, new journal, new goal. But the woman you're becoming doesn't wait for symbolic fresh starts. She trusts herself enough to begin again at 2:47 p.m. on a random Wednesday. She doesn't need the perfect conditions to act in alignment; she just needs a moment of honesty and one small choice. That's what separates the old story from the new one. The old story says, *Try again later.* Or, *Give up.* The new story says, *Begin again now.* Every time you begin again without waiting for a clean slate, you dismantle the narrative that you're someone who always quits. That's the heart of rewriting: you stop delaying your own life and start living inside it in real time.

Make Your Self-Trust Personal

And then comes the deepest layer—the part no one can do for you. You have to make your self-trust personal. Not driven by comparison, not shaped by what your friend is doing, not fueled by what strangers online say you should be capable of. Your self-trust identity must be rooted in your actual life, your actual nervous system, your actual capacity, your actual desires. If you base your self-trust on someone else's expectations, you're building a shaky foundation that will collapse under the weight of misalignment. The woman you're becoming keeps promises tailored to her reality. She honors her energy instead of fighting it. She builds credibility with herself in ways that feel like home, not like punishment. And because her promises fit her life, she can keep them. Keeping them reinforces her trust. And that trust becomes her identity.

This is the real rewrite. Not a new habit tracker. Not a new morning routine. Not a new set of rules. A new relationship with yourself. A new way of speaking to yourself. A new way of meeting yourself in the in-between moments when no one is applauding you for trying. A new way of catching the old story in the act and gently choosing something different. Rewriting the self-trust narrative is about stepping into authorship. It's when you stop being the character who reacts to life and start becoming the woman who creates it. It's when you stop believing the voice that tells you you're unreliable and start becoming the proof that you are not.

When you rewrite your self-trust narrative, you don't erase your past—you reclaim it. Every moment you abandoned yourself becomes fuel for the woman who refuses to do that anymore.

Every broken promise becomes motivation to build a stronger one. Every *I'll try again next week* becomes *I begin again now.* And every piece of evidence the old identity collected becomes a reminder that you are no longer living there. You're choosing differently. You're moving differently. You're building a life that requires the level of self-trust you're now willing to practice.

Rewrite your story, and you rewrite your identity. Rewrite your identity, and you rewrite your life. This is where *her* is born—not when everything is perfect, not when the fear is gone, but when you finally decide your word is worth keeping.

Protecting Your Self-Trust from Sabotage

Rebuilding self-trust is powerful, but protecting it is where the real transformation happens. Anyone can have a good day. Anyone can have a motivated morning. Anyone can keep one promise when the conditions are perfect. But the woman who keeps her word through the noise, through the temptations, through the pull of old patterns—that's the woman whose self-trust becomes unshakable. You cannot build a new identity while living in an environment designed for your old one. You can try, but it will drain you. It will exhaust you. It will convince you that you're failing when you're actually fighting a setup that was never built to help you rise. Protecting your self-trust is not about discipline; it's about removing the friction that pulls you back into who you used to be and intentionally creating support for the woman you're becoming.

Most self-sabotage doesn't look obvious. It's not always binge-eating, overspending, or ghosting your goals for weeks. More often, sabotage is subtle. It sounds like *I'll do it later* and *Five more minutes on my phone won't hurt*. It looks like keeping the notifications on when you promised yourself a break because you don't want to miss something. It looks like saying yes to a favor you didn't have space for. It looks like trying to fix everything at once and then burning out. Self-sabotage often hides inside the habits that feel harmless. But harmless habits still erode your self-trust when they take you away from the identity you're building.

Protecting your self-trust starts with honesty—brutal, loving honesty about the places you're still setting yourself up to fail. For most women, the phone is the first culprit. We tell ourselves we'll start the morning grounded and focused, but our phone is sitting on the nightstand begging to be checked the very first thing we wake up. The old identity thrives on distraction; the new identity thrives on intention. Deciding not to look at your phone right when you wake up is not a productivity hack—it's a self-trust boundary. It's saying, *I deserve a morning that isn't hijacked by everyone else's energy*. Screens are engineered to pull you away from yourself. You protect your self-trust by refusing to let them run your first hour of the day.

Then there's overcommitting, which is one of the most common ways women unintentionally break their own trust. When you say yes to everything, you end up abandoning yourself by default. Your schedule becomes so full of commitments to other people that you have no space to honor commitments to yourself. Every unnecessary yes becomes a quiet no to your own growth. Protecting your self-trust means pausing before you commit and asking, *Do I have the capacity for this?* not *Do I feel guilty saying no?*

> *The woman you're becoming understands that her energy is a resource, and protecting it is not selfish—it's strategic. When you protect your capacity, you protect your integrity.*

Another way self-sabotage sneaks in is through the physical spaces you live and work in. You may not realize how much your environment dictates your behavior until you try to build new habits inside a space that reflects an old identity. A cluttered counter whispers, *You never follow through*. A chaotic desk says, *You're already behind*. A messy room tells your brain you're unsafe, overwhelmed, and not ready to change. Protecting your self-trust doesn't mean you need a Pinterest-worthy home; it means you intentionally create environments that support follow-through instead of eroding it.

The smallest reset—clearing a nightstand, washing a sink full of dishes, setting out your clothes for the next morning—can be the difference between breaking your word and keeping it. You're not just cleaning a space; you're removing the excuses your old identity loves to hide behind.

Self-trust also requires protecting yourself from the people who drain your commitment to your own growth. Not everyone gets to walk beside you while you're rewriting your identity. Some people are so used to your old patterns that your growth will feel like a threat. Some will subtly pull you back into the version of you they're comfortable with. Some will joke about your habits or roll their eyes at your boundaries. And some will cheer for you but still expect you to meet their needs before your own. You don't have to cut everyone off to protect your self-trust, but you do have to become conscious of whose energy you let influence your choices. The woman you're becoming is deliberate about proximity. She doesn't apologize for prioritizing relationships that nourish the identity she is building.

One of the most overlooked forms of sabotage is keeping your promises too big. We think self-trust is built through grand gestures—huge goals, big commitments, intense routines. But most women break trust with themselves because the promises they make are unrealistic. They commit to too much too fast, and when they can't sustain it, they internalize it as failure. Protecting your self-trust means promising less so you can deliver more. Instead of committing to an hour at the gym, you commit to 10 minutes of movement. Instead of promising to meditate daily for 20 minutes, you promise 2 minutes. Instead of planning an elaborate morning routine, you anchor yourself in one nonnegotiable. This is not lowering your standards; it's lowering the barrier to entry. When you set yourself up to win, you teach your brain that your word can be trusted. Small wins become self-trust bricks. Stack enough bricks and you build a foundation.

Self-trust is also protected through routine—simple, grounding rhythms that remind your nervous system that you are safe, steady, and capable. Rituals aren't about the action itself; they're about the identity signal they send. When you wash your face at night instead of falling asleep in your makeup, you send the message that your well-being matters. When you journal for five minutes, you send the message that your thoughts deserve space. When you make your bed in the morning, you send the message that you are a woman who finishes the things she starts. Tiny rituals communicate to your brain and body, "I take myself seriously now." And that message becomes hard to ignore.

One of the most powerful ways to protect your self-trust is recognizing the difference between resistance and misalignment. Resistance is normal—every identity shift comes with it. Misalignment, however, is your body telling you that the promise you made doesn't belong to the woman you're becoming. Protecting your self-trust means learning to tell the difference.

For example, you tell yourself you're going to go to the gym after dinner. When the time comes, you feel resistance. You're tired, it feels inconvenient, part of you wants to stay on the couch. But you know you're going to feel so good when it's done. That's discomfort. That's the moment to move anyway, even if it's just showing up for 20 minutes.

Now compare that to this: you commit to waking up at 4:30 a.m. every day because you think you should. But every night you feel this heaviness about it. You dread going to bed because you know what's coming. It doesn't feel like a stretch. It feels like pressure. Like something in you is already bracing. That's not resistance. That's misalignment. And instead of forcing it, you adjust the commitment to something you can actually follow through on.

The old you ignored her body; the new you listens to it. Self-trust thrives where self-honesty lives.

Ultimately, protecting your self-trust is about making it harder to break your word and easier to keep it. You remove the obstacles that sabotage you. You strengthen the support that sustains you. You stop trying to rely on willpower alone and build structure, space, boundaries, and environments that make your follow-through feel natural. The woman you're becoming knows that trust isn't a feeling; it's a system. It's not built by accident. It's designed with intention.

When you protect your self-trust, you stop needing motivation to move. You stop waiting for the perfect moment. You stop thinking your life will change when you feel ready. You realize the truth: your life will change when you protect the version of you who is trying to rise. And once you learn how to guard your self-trust, you'll do anything to keep it—because nothing feels more powerful than becoming a woman who keeps her word.

This Is a Vote for Who I Am

You know the kind of choices in which no one else will know what you decide? The ones you could easily brush off with *I'll do it tomorrow* and move on with your day like it doesn't matter? The kind that looks small from the outside, but quietly builds or breaks trust with yourself?

A few years ago, I sat in my car outside an eye clinic with that exact choice staring me in the face. It wasn't the kind of moment that looks profound on Instagram. I had booked an eye appointment weeks earlier because headaches had been creeping back, and I knew I'd been overdue for a checkup. That morning, I woke up tired and unmotivated, telling myself I'd go as long as nothing else came up. Conveniently, everything came up. The kids were cranky. The dishes were piled high. My brain felt foggy. My old identity—professional escape artist—was already whispering the excuses I knew by heart: *you're too busy today. Just reschedule. It's not urgent. No one will care if you skip it.*

And I was right. No one would care. There would be no repercussions, no disappointed texts, no accountability from the outside world. Missing that appointment would've been invisible to everyone—except the woman I was trying to become.

So I drove there anyway. The whole time, that quiet tug-of-war played out in my chest: the part of me that wanted to keep my word and the part of me that wanted to slip back into the familiar comfort of avoidance. By the time I pulled into the parking lot, the latter was winning. I sat there debating, scrolling my phone, convincing myself that leaving was the logical choice. After all, I could rebook. I could go next week. I could do it when life felt less chaotic.

But as I started to turn the keys in the ignition, something in me paused. A flicker of awareness. A whisper that felt like truth: you've lived this moment a thousand times. You already know how this ends.

Because it wasn't about the appointment. It rarely is. It was about the story I'd been rehearsing for years—the story that said I didn't follow through, that I broke my own word more often than I kept it, that my needs were optional and everyone else's came first. The story that shaped my identity long before my actions ever did.

If I left that parking lot, I wouldn't just be skipping an appointment. I'd be voting for that old story again.

That was the moment everything snapped into focus. This tiny, boring choice held the same weight as every big decision I'd been trying to make. Every small action is a vote for who you are. Every kept promise is a brick of self-trust. Every broken one is a crack.

So I turned off the engine. I took a deep breath. And I walked inside.

Nothing miraculous happened in that waiting room. The fluorescent lights buzzed. A toddler cried three chairs down. An elderly man flipped through a magazine. It was the most ordinary scene in the world. But for me, it was a quiet revolution. Sitting in that chair was about proving to myself that I could be a woman who follows through even when it's inconvenient, even when no one is watching, even when the payoff isn't immediate.

Walking out afterward, something subtle but powerful had shifted inside me. A calm, grounded certainty: I can trust myself to do what I say I'm going to do. That certainty wasn't built in the appointment itself; it was built in all the micro-moments that led to it. The moment I didn't turn the car back on. The moment

I stepped out onto the pavement. The moment I checked in at the front desk. A series of tiny yeses to the woman I said I wanted to be.

This is what most people misunderstand about self-trust. It doesn't arrive in a breakthrough. It doesn't click into place after one big win. It's built like strength—incrementally, consistently, quietly. Every time you follow through, even when it seems trivial, you reinforce the identity you're trying to embody. And every time you abandon yourself, even in the smallest ways, you reinforce the identity you're trying to outgrow.

When women tell me they struggle with confidence, motivation, discipline, or consistency, what they're really saying is, "I don't trust myself yet." And that's not a flaw. It's a signal. It means your inner safety has been compromised by years of broken promises—to yourself. The good news is, rebuilding it doesn't require dramatic reinvention. It requires intention. Honesty. Micro-moments. Choices made when no one else is around to applaud you.

That day in the parking lot taught me something I've never forgotten: the world sees your big decisions, but your identity is shaped by your small ones. That's where she is born—in the split-second moments when you show up differently, when you decide the old you doesn't get the final say, when you choose integrity over convenience. That's when you prove to yourself, piece by piece, that you are trustworthy.

And as you strengthen that trust, something incredible happens. Your energy shifts. Your follow-through increases. Your confidence begins to feel inevitable. Because the woman who trusts herself moves differently. She speaks differently. She builds differently. Nothing external can rattle her as easily because she knows she can rely on herself to handle it.

This is the work that prepares you for everything that comes next. Trust isn't just the backbone of confidence—it's the foundation of embodiment. It's how you move from awareness to action, from intention to identity, from hoping you'll change to becoming the woman who does.

And that's where we go in Chapter 6.

When you start treating every decision—big or small—as a vote for who you are becoming, you stop trying to earn confidence and start embodying it. You stop performing smallness and start leading yourself into your next era. Because once you learn to trust yourself, deeply and honestly, *her* energy isn't something you chase. It's something you live.

Key Points

We covered a lot here, but this is what I want you to walk away with:

- The relationship you have with yourself—whether you believe your own word or not—decides everything.
- You don't become confident and then take action. You take action and then you build confidence.
- Sometimes the bravest thing you can do is slow the pace, not speed it up.
- You don't need to flawlessly execute every promise to build self-trust. You just need to start keeping one more promise to yourself today than you kept yesterday.
- Protecting your self-trust starts with honesty: brutal, loving honesty about the places you're still setting yourself up to fail.
- Your life will change when you protect the version of you who is trying to rise.

Chapter 6

Embodying Her Energy

I can still picture that bathroom like it's pressed into my memory. I was 10 years old, in fifth grade, getting ready for school the same way I did every morning. The bathroom had these old medicine cabinet mirrors that opened like little doors, and I swung them both out so I could see the back of my hair. That was my only intention—check the back, brush my teeth, grab my backpack. But then I turned my head just a little too far, and the angle shifted, and my breath stopped. The reflection staring back at me wasn't the one I thought I knew. I froze, toothbrush still in my hand, foam on my lips, staring at this side profile I had never seen before in my entire 10 years of life. And there it was: the curve in my nose, the little hump I had somehow gone a whole decade without ever noticing.

For a moment, I genuinely thought it had to be the light. Or a weird shadow. Or the mirror warping. I tilted my head forward, then back, side to side, checking the reflection again and again, desperate for it to disappear. But it didn't. No matter how I moved, the hump was there. Permanent. Real. Mine.

It's strange how a single second can rearrange your entire sense of self. Up until that moment, my nose was just a nose. Something that sat on my face and did its job. But in the span of a heartbeat, it became the thing I was suddenly terrified everyone else had seen before I did. Something I needed to monitor, hide, fix. Something that made me feel exposed in a way I didn't have the vocabulary for yet.

I walked into school that day and for the first time in my life, I felt painfully self-conscious. Every whisper felt suspicious. Every laugh felt pointed. Every time someone looked at me, I wondered if they were staring at the very thing I had discovered that morning. I became acutely aware of angles—how I stood, how I turned, how I smiled. In every photo from that point forward, my chin dipped just a bit, my smile adjusted just slightly, my posture tightened like I was trying to camouflage myself without anyone noticing. Ten-year-old me couldn't explain it, but she understood one thing instantly: she wanted that nose gone.

And so began the dream of the "new nose." I would go back to that same mirror and cup my hand over the hump, imagining what it would look like if the line from the bridge to the tip was perfectly straight. I'd imagine how different I'd feel, how much more beautiful I'd seem, how confidence might finally feel natural instead of something I had to rehearse. I imagined walking into rooms and not questioning how I was being seen, just feeling like I belonged there. In my 10-year-old mind, that nose was the difference between invisibility and belonging.

Then life happened, and the insecurity deepened. Losing my mom at 15 cracked something in me, something that made every insecurity feel louder, sharper, harder to escape. Grief rearranged my world and left me carrying this invisible heaviness that said, *You're on your own now.* And somehow, that message tangled itself with the insecurity that started in the mirror that morning. It became one belief: something about me is broken.

So the nose obsession wasn't just about beauty anymore. It became a symbol. A placeholder for everything I thought was wrong with me. All the times I compared myself to girls who seemed effortless. All the years I felt small, unchosen, unworthy. Fixing the hump started to feel like the only way to erase the broken girl I saw in myself.

By the time I was 20, the fantasy had turned into a plan. In the summer of 2013, I took my first job up north in the Yukon, driving a rock truck and feeding a gold mine plant with a frontend loader. It was rugged work—dust caked under your nails, boots sinking into mud, the smell of diesel settling into your clothes—but I didn't care. Every 12-hour shift, every late-night haul, every freezing morning felt like a step closer to the version of me I was so desperate to become. I wasn't saving money for adventure or for a new start. I was saving for a new face, a new identity, a new chance at feeling worthy.

Every paycheck I deposited, I'd run the numbers in my head. How much longer until I could afford it? How close was I to finally fixing the one thing I was convinced held me back from feeling confident, beautiful, normal? It didn't matter that I was living in the wilderness or working shifts that made my bones ache. I had one mission: get the surgery. Fix the nose. Fix me. Be complete.

And as soon as I had enough, I booked it. Ten thousand dollars—money I had worked for, sweated for, sacrificed for—gone in an instant. But I didn't hesitate. I remember thinking, This is the best money I will ever spend. This is the day my life will finally turn around.

The day of the surgery, I sat in the doctor's office with my heart thundering in my chest. I was this strange cocktail of terrified and elated, like I was standing on the edge of a cliff and believing with everything in me that the jump would lead somewhere better. I kept whispering to myself, *This is it. This is the moment everything changes. This is the moment I become something better.*

Afterward, I spent weeks with bandages on my face, waiting for the big reveal. I would lie awake imagining the moment the doctor removed the tape, imagining the rush of finally seeing a version of myself I believed I could love. I counted down the days like it was Christmas morning.

And then, finally, the bandages came off. I turned toward the mirror, and for the first time since that day in the bathroom at 10 years old, I saw a nose without the hump.

Did I look different? Yes. Did I feel prettier? Absolutely. Did I feel changed? In the first few seconds, yes—it was intoxicating. A high. A hit of relief I had been chasing for more than a decade. I remember touching the bridge of my nose with shaky fingers, marveling at the straight line where the bump used to be.

But then I stepped away from the mirror. And that's when it hit me.

I still felt like the same girl.

The same doubts. The same insecurities. The same ache of unworthiness that had rooted itself in me years earlier. I realized, with a kind of heaviness I wasn't ready for, that I had placed an impossible amount of hope inside that surgery. I had believed that removing a hump would remove the grief, the shame, the self-criticism, the quiet craving to be enough. But it didn't.

My face had changed. My confidence hadn't.

That's when the truth landed with a force I'll never forget: *you cannot outsource confidence.* You can't swipe a card and buy it. You can't surgically install it. You can't hope it arrives in a package or a procedure. Because confidence isn't created by the outside world—it's created in the way you choose to show up inside your own skin.

> *Until you decide who you are, nothing external can make you feel like enough.*

That realization didn't make me regret the surgery. It just made me understand it differently. It wasn't a fix. It wasn't a cure. It was a mirror—one that showed me clearly that the glow-up I was craving wasn't about changing my face. It was about changing the story I was living inside.

That's the shift this chapter is here to create for you. This is the moment when you stop waiting for confidence to come from the outside—a paycheck, a compliment, a new wardrobe, a perfect routine—and start building it from the inside out. This is when you begin embodying *her* energy not through aesthetics or perfection, but through intention, presence, and identity. Through how you visualize yourself. Through the environments you build around you. Through the energy you choose to carry, even on the days you feel wobbly.

Because once you embody *her* energy, the outside world doesn't get to decide how confident you feel anymore.

You do. And that one shift changes everything.

The Truth About Energy and Identity

A lot of women think confidence lives in the things we do. The clothes we wear. The way we style our hair. The goals we hit. The routines we perfect. But confidence doesn't live in any of that. Confidence lives in the energy underneath those choices, and the wildest part is that most of us walk through our entire lives never realizing how much of our identity is being broadcast long before we ever say a word.

You know this instinctively. You've met women who walk into a room and immediately shift the atmosphere without trying. They aren't necessarily the most beautiful. They aren't the loudest, or the richest, or the ones wearing head-to-toe designer. But their presence holds weight. There is a steadiness to them, a groundedness, a quiet certainty that makes people look twice. It's not anything they're doing. It's how they're being. That's identity at work. That's energy.

Energy Doesn't Lie

Energy is the most honest expression of who you believe you are. You can put on the outfit. You can repeat the affirmations. You can craft the perfect caption. But if your identity is still rooted in *I'm not enough*, your energy will betray you every single time. Identity isn't on the surface. Identity is in the way you breathe when you walk into a room you're not sure you belong in. It's in the way your shoulders fold or expand when someone compliments you. It's in the way your voice tightens when you're afraid of sounding stupid or the way your eyes drop when you don't want to take up too much space.

Energy doesn't lie. And energy doesn't wait for external validation. That's why you can spot a woman who's trying to act confident versus a woman who is confident. The first performs it. The second embodies it.

For years, I lived in the performance. I didn't have the language for it back then, but my entire existence was built on trying to avoid being seen "wrong." I walked into grocery stores with my head down. I whispered my order at restaurants as if taking up too much vocal space was a crime. I second-guessed my laughter, my posture, my volume, my opinions. I was constantly shape-shifting into whatever version of me felt safest in the moment—hoping no one would notice how deeply I didn't belong to myself yet. That's what happens when your identity is built on survival instead of self-trust. Your energy shrinks to match the story you've believed the longest.

When I finally started doing real identity work, I began noticing something I had never put words to before: the version of me I dreamed of becoming had an entirely different energy than the one I was living in every day. In my mind, she wasn't cautious. She wasn't apologetic. She wasn't scanning the room trying to manage everyone's perception of her. She walked with a kind of ease, a calm confidence that said, I trust myself to be here. Even before she knew all the answers. Even before anything external proved she deserved it. She led with energy, not evidence.

That realization was the beginning of everything shifting for me. I didn't need to wait for the right body, the right wardrobe, the right career milestone, or the right chapter of my healing to feel like her. I needed to begin carrying the energy of the woman I said I was becoming, even when the external parts of my life still looked half-built. Energy leads identity. Identity leads behavior. Behavior leads results. And every time I showed up with a slightly expanded energy—standing a little taller, slowing my breath before speaking, making eye contact instead of darting away—I was teaching my nervous system a new story: I belong here.

This is the part most women miss. You don't become her and then embody her energy. You embody her energy, and that's what helps you become her. Your energy shifts first. Your identity shifts next. And your life rearranges itself around that shift.

Your Energy Tells People How to Treat You

But there's a deeper truth underneath this, and it's the one that changed me the most: the way you see yourself is the way the world learns to see you. If you walk into a room believing you're too much, too loud, too inexperienced, too unqualified, people will feel that from you before you open your mouth. If you walk in believing you're allowed to take up space, that you can hold a conversation, that your presence adds something real—people will pick up on that, too.

Your energy teaches others how to treat you.

And here's the part that used to blow my mind: most of the women you admire aren't more confident than you. They've just practiced being themselves longer. Their energy is trained. Their identity is rehearsed. They've made a thousand tiny decisions to stop abandoning themselves in the moments when it used to feel easiest to shrink. That's why they feel magnetic. They're not perfect. They're present. They're not performing confidence—they're inhabiting it.

Identity and energy function like a loop. What you believe creates how you show up. How you show up becomes proof of what you believe. Eventually, you stop playing the role of the shy girl, the insecure girl, the girl who waits for permission, and you start breathing like the woman who trusts herself. The woman who doesn't beg for safety because she has learned how to create it internally. The woman who doesn't ask if she's allowed to take up space because she knows she already is the space.

Your Energy Is Powerful

This is where energy becomes your greatest asset. Because when you learn how to shift your energy with intention, you stop outsourcing confidence to the outside world. You stop waiting for someone else to choose you first. You stop waiting for perfect timing. You start showing up like *her*—not someday, but now. And once you've felt what that energy feels like in your body, you can't unknow it. You can't go back to the version of you who waits for evidence to prove she's allowed to rise.

The real secret is this: your energy is already powerful. It always has been. You've just spent years dimming it to survive. Now, you're learning how to turn it back on. Through the way you choose to see yourself. Through the energy you decide to lead with. Through the woman you practice being before the world believes it . . . but eventually because you believed it first.

That's the truth about energy and identity: they're not separate. They mirror each other. And once you master that relationship, nothing in your life stays small.

Identity Visualization

Before life got heavy, before grief rearranged the blueprint of who I thought I was allowed to become, I used to daydream without limits. As a kid, my imagination was its own world: bright, detailed, vivid. I didn't just picture the things I wanted; I could almost feel them. But after my mom died, those daydreams shifted. They went from expansive to restricted. From possibility to limitation. From, who could I become to who am I kidding? Visualization slowly turned into forecasting disappointment. I didn't even realize it was happening. I just stopped imagining a future that felt big.

And yet—even in the darkest stretch of my teenage years and early 20s—there was always this quiet image that kept sneaking through. A flicker. A picture that made no logical sense based on who I believed myself to be at the time. I didn't call her anything back then, but now I know exactly who she was: the woman I would eventually become. The one I now refer to as *her*.

Even when I couldn't access hope, I could still access her silhouette.

I would picture walking into a room with my shoulders soft, not tense. My head held naturally high instead of tucked down. I'd imagine what it would feel like to speak without rehearsing every word in my mind first. I'd imagine laughing loudly—something I did all the time as a kid, but somewhere along the line convinced myself it took up too much space. I would picture her in a job she loved, not one she lied her way into just to survive. I'd picture her living near the water, even though at the time I couldn't afford a new pair of jeans, let alone an island lifestyle. She felt impossibly far away, but she felt consistently real.

That's the thing about visualization that most people misunderstand: it's not about pretending you're a different person. It's about remembering who you are beneath the layers of fear, doubt, and survival patterns you've collected along the way. Your imagination isn't delusional—it's directional. It shows you the identity your subconscious already recognizes as yours.

But when most women try to visualize, they treat it like wishing. They close their eyes and hope something changes. They try to picture the dream life but feel like they're lying to themselves. They imagine the version of them who has everything they want, and instead of feeling inspired, they feel defeated. Because in the back of their mind, they're reinforcing the gap: *here I am . . . and there she is. Two different worlds.*

That isn't visualization. That's self-rejection in a prettier outfit.

Real visualization—the kind that rewires identity—is not about imagining a life you don't believe you can have. It's about practicing the energy of the woman you're becoming until your body recognizes it as familiar, safe, and true. It's about making your nervous system comfortable with expansion instead of treating it like danger. It's like rehearsing a role you were born to play but somehow forgot.

Your brain doesn't know the difference between what's real and what's vividly imagined. That's why you can picture a stressful conversation and your heart rate spikes. Or imagine yourself on a beach and genuinely feel calmer. The body responds to imagery as if it's happening now. That's why you get stuck in cycles: if you keep visualizing everything that could go wrong, your body lives like it's happening already. But when you start visualizing HER—who she is, how she moves, what she carries—you start training your nervous system to stop panicking at the idea of change.

You're not wishing. You're rewiring.

There's a season I still think about often—the one right after I left the Yukon. That was my identity earthquake. Everything felt uncertain, half-built, unstable. I had no clue what the next chapter looked like. All I knew was that the old version of me wasn't coming with me. And during that season, visualization wasn't cute or inspirational—it was survival. It gave me something to hold when I didn't have anything tangible yet.

I'd sit in my tiny apartment with my journal and picture the version of me who had her feet on solid ground. What her mornings felt like. How she made decisions. How she treated herself. How confidently she said no when something wasn't aligned. How she spoke up in conversations instead of shrinking. I'd picture her driving to the ocean just because she wanted to. I'd picture her with a business she loved, not knowing that one day I'd build an entire world that helps other women find *her*, too.

And here's the wildest part: the more I pictured her, the more I realized she wasn't some fantasy I needed to earn my way into. She wasn't a stranger or an invented persona. She was me—without the layers. Without the fear. Without the outdated identity scripts. Visualization wasn't about creating her. It was about remembering her.

That's why this practice is so powerful. The more you rehearse her energy in your mind, the easier it becomes to embody her in real life. Suddenly, walking into a room confidently doesn't feel impossible: your nervous system has experienced it a hundred times through visualization. Setting a boundary doesn't feel terrifying: you've imagined yourself doing it enough that it feels familiar. Posting online doesn't trigger a spiral: you've rehearsed the energy of being seen so many times that your body no longer interprets visibility as danger.

Visualization makes the unfamiliar familiar. And once something feels familiar, it feels possible.

So here's what I want you to try. Instead of visualizing from the outside in—what she owns, what she looks like, what she's achieved—I want you to visualize from the inside out. See her energy first. How she carries herself. How she speaks. How she breathes. How she self-soothes when she feels overwhelmed. How she moves through her day with grounded confidence instead of frantic survival.

Then imagine stepping into her skin. Borrow her breath. Let your shoulders fall into her posture. Imagine the way she holds eye contact. Imagine what it feels like to answer the question "So what do you do?" without shrinking. Imagine her self-respect, her discipline, her honesty, her softness, her power—all of it living in your body, because it already does.

Stay there for a minute. Let your body feel it. Let your nervous system absorb it. Let that version of you become familiar, not foreign.

Visualization isn't about escaping your reality. It's how you prime yourself for a new one. It's how you rehearse the identity you're stepping into so that when real-life moments ask you to rise, your body doesn't glitch or resist—it recognizes the role. It steps forward because it has been practicing.

One day, you'll catch yourself in the middle of something ordinary—getting dressed, talking to a friend, walking into a room—and you'll realize: you're not trying to visualize her anymore. You're not imagining what she would do. You're doing it. You've become the woman you used to close your eyes to picture.

And that's the real magic of visualization: when you practice *being* her long enough, you stop trying to *become* her.

You remember you already are *her.*

Environment as Proof

You eventually notice it: you're not just tweaking habits or fixing routines. You're rebuilding the world you wake up inside every morning. The room you move through, the noise you allow in, the tiny cues that either drag you back into who you were or nudge you toward who you are becoming.

Your environment is always shaping you, whether you realize it or not. Every counter, every closet, every notification, every playlist, every pile, every voice, every room—you are absorbing messages from all of it before you even realize it's happening. Your environment is either reinforcing your past or reflecting your future. And most women are trying to step into a new identity while standing in spaces that hold the energy of the version of them they're trying to outgrow.

I learned this slowly, almost accidentally. I used to believe I was just "messy" or "lazy" or "disorganized." But when I started doing identity work, I realized the truth: I had designed a world that matched the girl who didn't trust herself. The girl who didn't believe she could rise. The girl who felt safest staying small. My spaces reflected what I expected of myself, and I had never expected anything more.

My closet was full of clothes that made me disappear. Oversized hoodies and worn-out leggings that said, *Blend in. Don't draw attention.* My nightstand was cluttered with half-finished books and receipts and things I kept meaning to deal with. My phone was filled with accounts that drained me. My kitchen often mirrored the overwhelm I felt inside: half-done tasks everywhere, reinforcing the belief that I never finished anything. I didn't realize it then, but I was living in a museum dedicated to the outdated version of me.

And every morning, without saying a word, my environment whispered, *This is who you are.*

But once I started doing the deeper work, once I started building self-trust again, once I began embodying *her* energy even in tiny ways, I couldn't unsee the impact of my surroundings. That's when it clicked for me: your environment is a mirror, and it will always reflect the identity you expect yourself to live inside.

So instead of trying to force myself into new habits through sheer willpower, I started redesigning the world around me to support the woman I was choosing to become. I didn't do it all at once. There was no big makeover moment or anything drastic. It was small but intentional shifts—tiny upgrades that signaled to my nervous system, *We're living differently now.*

One of the biggest shifts began in my mornings. You know the story: the robe laid out, the candle ready, the kettle filled the night before. That wasn't about aesthetics or some Pinterest version of wellness. It was environment as identity engineering. When I woke up at 5 a.m., groggy and tempted to roll over and run from my own promises, my environment said, *No. We're already in motion.* There was no decision left to negotiate. The robe was waiting. The candle was waiting. My journal was waiting. My future self had already set the morning in motion.

> *That's what* her *environment does. It removes the friction between who you've been and who you're becoming.*

I started looking at everything that way. My closet shifted first. I got rid of pieces that made me shrink and kept the ones that made me feel like her, the ones that changed how I carried myself. Shirts I stood taller in. Jeans that made me walk differently. Clothes that felt like a woman who trusts herself.

Then came my phone. I unfollowed accounts that fed my insecurity or reinforced an identity I was tired of rehearsing. I curated my feed like a mood board for the life I was stepping into: women who inspired me, spaces that expanded me, messages that aligned with the energy I wanted to calibrate to.

Even my playlists changed. I stopped listening to music that kept me stuck in old emotional patterns and started filling my ears with sounds that made me feel alive, capable, softer, stronger. Small detail, huge impact.

I decluttered my physical space because the piles made my nervous system feel like I was falling behind before the day even started. I cleared surfaces so my mind had space to think. I lit candles not for the ambiance but because every time I struck a match, it felt like I was signaling to myself, *I'm creating a life I'm proud of.* This was about creating an environment that reflected the truth of who I already was underneath the noise.

You don't create *her* identity in your head. You create it through your world. When you intentionally shape your environment to support the woman you're becoming, you make it easier to show up as her. You make it easier to follow through. You make it easier to stay connected to your standards, your integrity, your dreams. You make it easier to keep your promises. You make it easier to choose yourself without a tug-of-war.

You take *her* from a concept to a lived experience.

Your environment eventually stops feeling like something you curated. It starts feeling like home. One day you wake up and realize you haven't fought yourself in the morning in weeks. You walk into your closet and everything you touch feels aligned with who you are. You sit down at your desk and feel grounded, not overwhelmed. Your surroundings quietly but powerfully remind you, *This is who I am now.*

That's the power of your environment. It's proof. It turns the invisible identity work into something tangible. You see it. You feel it. You live in it. You can't deny it because it's right in front of you. Your spaces become evidence of your evolution.

You don't need a perfect home or a big budget or a Pinterest-worthy office to do this. You just need intention. One corner of a room. One shelf. One drawer. One ritual. One playlist. One boundary. One habit that supports *her* instead of sabotaging her.

Every piece of your environment is either pulling you backward or pulling you forward. When you design your world to reflect your next-level self, you create a life that constantly nudges you into alignment. You create a world that makes it harder to abandon yourself and easier to become the woman you've been imagining all along.

Energetic Alignment in Real Life

It doesn't happen when everything is calm and put together. It happens in the middle of real life, when things feel messy, and you still choose to show up differently. Energetic alignment is not a mood. It's not something you tap into only when you're rested, inspired, and ready. Alignment is a practice. It's choosing *her* in the middle of your very real life, with your very real responsibilities, even when the moment feels far from ideal.

One of the biggest misconceptions women carry is that aligned energy has to feel next level. But more often than not, it looks like choosing a different response than the one your old identity has rehearsed for years. It looks like catching yourself in a familiar spiral and pivoting instead of drowning. It looks like staying with yourself instead of abandoning yourself in the hard moments.

I'll never forget the night that taught me this lesson in the most unfiltered way. I was in the thick of motherhood. Maddie was three, Rhett was two, and the entire house felt like a pressure cooker of noise and need. Both kids were crying, the new puppy was losing his mind over something imaginary (a puppy, I know, *add more to the chaos, Alicia*), the heat was unbearable, and every part of me felt stretched thin and close to snapping. My hair was sticking to the back of my neck, sweat running down my spine, and it felt like the walls were closing in.

Old me would have spiraled. She would have collapsed into self-pity, convinced she wasn't cut out for any of it. She would have repeated the same internal script: *Why is everything so hard for me?*

Why can't I handle life the way other women do? She would have let the moment confirm every fear she carried about not being enough.

But that night, something different happened. In the middle of the chaos, I felt a stillness come over me. A tiny pause where I could feel two choices sitting in front of me: shrink into the identity I'd known or rise into the one I'd been practicing. It wasn't inspiring on the surface. It wasn't empowering in the social media quote kind of way. It was gritty. Exhausting. Real.

I took a deep breath and asked myself quietly, *If I were* her—*the woman I'm becoming, the mother I want my kids to remember—how would she handle this moment?* Not perfectly. Not calmly. But with presence. With steadiness. With a refusal to abandon herself.

So I picked up my son. I held my daughter close. I turned on the fan. I handled the moment without collapsing into the story that I wasn't capable. And when the house finally quieted and both kids were asleep and the dog was chewing on his toy, I realized something: embodiment had just happened—in the heat of real life. In the moment when it mattered most.

That's energetic alignment. Not the absence of chaos, but the way you lead yourself *inside* it.

And you experience moments like this every day—far smaller than two screaming kids, but equally identity shaping. They happen in the checkout line at the grocery store when you choose to stand with confidence instead of shrinking your presence. They happen when someone asks where you want to eat and you answer honestly instead of saying, "I don't care, whatever works." They happen when your instinct is to apologize for taking up space, and instead you hold your tone steady. They happen when you're tempted to ghost on a promise to yourself, but you take the small action anyway.

Most people never realize how many micro-moments of energy are shaping their entire identity. They write them off as nothing—too small to matter—but they matter more than anything. Because energetic alignment is a loop. Every time you choose *her* in real time, you send your nervous system a tiny but powerful message: *this is who I am now*. And your body starts adapting to that new identity the same way it adapts to repetition in the gym. Reps build strength. Reps create familiarity. Reps make the movement easier.

And the beautiful, frustrating, miraculous thing about energetic alignment is this: your body will resist it at first. Even when it's aligned. Even when it's right. Even when it's what you want. Because your nervous system is designed to protect you, not evolve you. It interprets "new" as unsafe. Even when the old identity was the one hurting you. So when you first start practicing *her*, your heart might race. Your palms might sweat. Your voice might shake. You might feel silly, dramatic, or exposed. That's not a sign you're doing it wrong—it's a sign you're breaking the pattern.

One day you'll walk into a room without overthinking where to stand. You'll speak without rehearsing. You'll say no without spiraling. You'll post the thing online without waiting for permission. You'll trust your intuition without polling anyone else first. And you'll catch yourself thinking, *Oh my god . . . this is me now*.

The fear didn't disappear—your energy just finally caught up with the identity you've been practicing.

And the world responds. People notice before you do. "You seem different." "There's something about you lately." "I love your vibe." They can't name it, but your energy is speaking before you open your mouth. That's the power of alignment. It makes you unforgettable without performing. It makes you magnetic without trying. It turns *her* from a version you visualize into a woman you live as.

Energetic alignment is showing up even when it would be easier to shrink. It's the quiet, ordinary, private moments where you choose your future self over your familiar past.

It's the evidence that identity work isn't happening in your journal. It's happening in real time.

The Amplifier, Not the Mask

For most of my life, I treated beauty rituals like rescue missions. The spray tans, the lash extensions, the hair appointments—they weren't fun back then. They were lifelines. I wasn't doing them because they made me feel expressed or playful. I was doing them because I didn't think I was enough without them. Every appointment was an attempt to outrun the version of me I still didn't know how to live with. I believed if I could look polished enough, perfect enough, pretty enough, maybe I'd finally feel the confidence I kept chasing.

But once I learned the difference between embodying confidence and outsourcing it, everything changed. Suddenly those same rituals weren't about fixing myself. They were about expressing myself. They stopped being a mask and started being an amplifier.

The shift was subtle at first. It happened on a random day after I'd been practicing *her* energy for a while: micro-decisions, aligned choices, showing up in real moments even when it stretched me. I had booked a spray tan and a hair extension appointment back to back. I'd done both a hundred times before, but that day felt different.

Standing half naked in that freezing little spray tan room, in those tragic disposable underwear, with a stranger directing me to "turn to the left . . . chin up . . . now the right," I realized I didn't feel desperate. Old me would've been silently praying, please let this make me feel beautiful. Please let this be the thing that finally makes me enough. But that day, I wasn't begging the tan to hand me confidence. I already had it. I already felt solid in my skin before the color ever hit it.

Later, sitting in the salon chair as my stylist clipped in fresh extensions, I caught myself grinning. It wasn't the hair. *It was me.* The extensions weren't fixing me. They were simply highlighting a version of myself I had already claimed internally. When the stylist asked if I wanted extra volume, "more drama," old me would've hesitated. Worried about being too much. Worried about attention. Worried about judgment. But *her* energy didn't hesitate. "Yes," I said. "Give me the drama."

And the second she spun that chair around, I laughed. I finally recognized myself. For the first time in my life, the outside finally matched who I felt like inside. It wasn't the hair that made me confident. It was that I had finally become the kind of woman who didn't need the hair *to* be confident.

That's when I understood the truth: external rituals only ever amplify the energy you already hold. If you're rooted in self-trust, alignment, and identity, the blowout, the makeup, the outfit, the tan—they don't create confidence. They turn the volume up on it. They give your embodied energy a louder microphone. But if you're operating from insecurity, from the old story, from the tiny, shrinking identity you've lived inside for years, the externals become a mask you're terrified to take off.

When I left the salon that day, I stopped at the grocery store. Nothing fancy—just grabbing pull-ups, coffee creamer, and whatever else motherhood requires at random. But people looked at me differently. It wasn't the tan or the hair. It was the shift in how I was showing up, and the whole room felt it. I wasn't shrinking. I wasn't hiding. I wasn't tugging at my clothes or checking my reflection in every chrome surface. I was walking through a fluorescent-lit grocery store like I belonged there, like it was my space. The difference wasn't what I looked like. It was the way I saw myself. That's embodiment. Not the perfect image. Not the curated aesthetic. Not the flawless presentation. Embodiment is who you are when you're bagging groceries at 7 p.m. on a Tuesday. Embodiment is who you are when no one is looking. It's in your walk, your posture, your presence, your tone. It's energy first, aesthetics second.

I need you to hear this in the deepest way: you can enjoy every beauty ritual on earth without making them a crutch. You can love your lashes, your nails, your hair appointments, your tan, your favorite outfit. It stops being about fixing or hiding and starts being about expression. That's the difference between the girl who stood in that cosmetic surgery clinic thinking a $10,000 surgery would save her, and the woman walking confidently through a grocery store simply enjoying her fresh hair extensions. One was chasing confidence from the outside in. The other was amplifying confidence from the inside out.

This chapter, at its core, is your permission slip to stop waiting for the external world to hand you the confidence you're meant to claim. To stop thinking you need to earn your glow before you show up in it. To stop outsourcing your power to anything that can be washed off, wiped off, cut off, or taken away.

Because the moment you decide to embody *her* energy, everything external becomes optional, playful, expressive—never required. The tan, the hair, the makeup, the outfit, the scent—they become accessories to a confidence you already own. Tools that enhance, not tools that save.

When you live from this place, you walk into every room—salon, grocery store, meeting, date night, school pickup—already knowing who you are. Already anchored. Already whole. No stylist, no product, no procedure can give you that. But once you have it, they can absolutely make *her* louder.

That's the glow no one can take from you. Because it doesn't come from the outside. It radiates from the woman you already are.

Key Points

If you've been nodding along, here's what you actually need to hold on to:

- You cannot outsource confidence. It's created in the way you choose to show up inside your own skin.
- The way you see yourself is the way the world learns to see you.
- Visualization makes the unfamiliar familiar. It helps you rehearse the identity you're stepping into.
- Your environment is a mirror. And it will always reflect the identity you expect yourself to live inside.
- When you intentionally shape your environment to support the woman you're becoming, you make it easier to show up as her.
- External rituals only ever amplify the energy you already hold—they don't create confidence.

Part Two

CLOSER AND REFLECTION

Part Two Closer: Becoming Her Now

By the time you reach this point in the book, you've already done something most women never give themselves permission to do: you stopped waiting for the perfect moment and started meeting yourself where you are. You faced the parts of you that were tired of pretending. You walked into rooms, memories, and truths you've spent years avoiding. You chose support before collapse. You rebuilt pieces of yourself you assumed were too far gone. You started practicing the kind of self-trust that grows in the dark, not the spotlight. And you began embodying the energy of a woman you once believed you had to earn the right to become.

That's the real glow-up. Not the results, not the evidence, not the perfect follow through. The glow-up is getting honest about who you've been and choosing, in small ways, to stop abandoning yourself for her. The glow-up is showing up even when your voice shakes. It's building proof where there used to be doubt. It's aligning your environment, your energy, and your actions with a version of you who no longer shrinks for anyone—not even your past self.

Part Two wasn't about becoming perfect. It wasn't about "fixing yourself" or arriving at some imaginary healed version of you who never spirals or slips. It was about remembering that healing isn't a prerequisite for your life—it's the process of living it. It was about learning how to stand with yourself in motion, not months from now, not when everything calms down, but right now, inside the imperfect moments that shape your identity more than any milestone ever could.

And now comes the part most women never reach: the part where you live it.

Identity work isn't meant to stay in the journal or the morning routine. It's meant to breathe inside your relationships, your voice, your choices, your presence, your life. Part Three is where the internal becomes external. Where the woman you've been practicing in private gets to show up in the real world. Where confidence stops being a concept and becomes a way of moving. Where worthiness becomes the baseline you lead from, not the finish line you chase.

You're ready for that. You've built the foundation. You've met yourself honestly, rebuilt your trust, and stepped into your energy with intention. Part Three is where that work comes alive.

The next version of you isn't waiting. She's already here—and now you get to live in your magic.

Part Two Reflection: Become the Woman You're Building

Before you turn the page and move into the next part of this book, pause. You've just walked through the messy, beautiful middle of becoming—the part no one glamorizes, the part where real change happens. You've met the version of you who didn't wait for rock bottom to get support. You've rebuilt trust with a woman you spent years abandoning. You've practiced showing up in a way your past self never believed you could. You've stepped into your energy, your presence, your identity in small but life-altering ways. None of this is subtle. None of this is accidental. And none of this is temporary.

This is your moment to breathe before you rise again. To sit with the fact that you have been doing the work—not in dramatic declarations, but in the small, private choices that no one else sees. You've been rewriting your story one micro-decision at a time. You've been laying the foundation for a life you're finally ready to live inside of. Let yourself take that in.

As you sit here, ask yourself these questions without rushing, without apologizing, and without pretending. You don't need to be "ready." You just need to be honest.

- Where did I show up for myself in ways the old me never could have?
- What did rebuilding my self-trust look like in real life—and what proof do I now have that I can count on myself?
- What energy am I done carrying into my future—and what energy am I choosing instead?

These questions aren't asking for a performance. They're asking for your truth. They're mirrors for the parts of you that have quietly grown stronger, steadier, braver while no one was watching. They remind you that the woman you're becoming isn't a fantasy—she's already being built through every self-loyal choice you've made so far.

Now choose one embodiment action—just one—that aligns with *her*. Not a makeover. Not a full routine overhaul. One grounded move that says, *I trust myself now.* Maybe it's the way you speak in a meeting. Maybe it's putting your phone in another room so you can hear your own thoughts. Maybe it's showing up to your morning the way the woman you're becoming would. Whatever it is, let it be something that reinforces the identity you've been practicing, not the one you're outgrowing.

You don't need to perfect anything before moving forward. You just need to take one step that proves you're not waiting for a new life to begin—you're building it.

And as you close this part and walk into the next—the part where you stop trying to become her and start *living* as her—carry this with you:

I can trust myself to lead now.

Because you can. And when you do, everything expands.

Part Three

LIVING IT, OWNING IT, EXPANDING IT

You don't notice it at first—the softening, the steadying, the recalibration. But one day you realize you're not forcing the growth anymore. You're simply living it. You're not reaching for her—you are embodying her.

That's what Part Three is about. Not the climb. Not the healing. Not the unraveling. This is the part where your life starts to meet you at the level of your self-trust, where the choices you once had to think your way into become instinct, where your voice feels clearer, where your energy feels cleaner, where your days begin to feel like something you're in, not something you're chasing.

This isn't the "one-day" version of you. This is the real-time version—the woman who has done the inner work, rewired the old stories, and built the identity strong enough to hold the life she wants. Part Three is where you learn to live in the identity you've built. To take up space without shrinking. To let good things stay. To lead yourself with steadiness instead of urgency. To build a life that reflects the woman you've become instead of the girl you used to be.

This is where your life expands because *you* expanded. This is where you stop asking, *Am I ready?* and start asking, *What feels true for me now?* You're not stepping into *her* anymore. You're living from her. Welcome to Part Three, where everything you've built starts to show up in the way you think, choose, breathe, love, and lead. The part where life becomes something you get to shape, not something you react to. The part where you stop waiting for magic and realize you are the magic in your life.

Chapter 7

The Moment Everything Shifted

It was a Monday night in the middle of one of those long stretches when the days all blur together. The kids had preschool and swimming lessons that day so bedtime wasn't a fight in the slightest. They were asleep, the dishes were done, and the house had settled into that rare quiet that only exists after bedtime. I remember standing in the kitchen wiping down the counter for absolutely no reason, the way you do when your mind is restless but you can't quite place why. Everything felt normal. Nothing about that night felt like a moment that would mark me.

Then my phone rang, and my brother's name lit up across the screen.

Now, here's the thing: Terence calling is never alarming. We talk about everything. We always have. My mom drilled into us from the time we were tiny that no matter what happened in the world, we'd always have each other. And she was right. He's not just my brother—he's my teammate, my sounding board, my built-in best friend. So when he FaceTimes or calls, it's usually something pointless or hilarious or something he knows only I would appreciate.

So when I saw his name, I didn't tense up. I didn't brace. I didn't prepare for anything heavy. I answered the phone with some teasing comment, something like, "Hey loser!"—the kind of effortless sibling banter we've had our whole lives.

Except he didn't laugh. He didn't match my tone. He didn't even try.

He just said, "Have you talked to Dad today?"

It was the way he said it. Quiet. Careful. Like he was holding something fragile in his mouth and didn't want to break it. My whole body went still. I said no. And then "Why?"

And that's when he told me. He said Dad's oxygen had been dipping into the 70s. The 70s. That he'd looked gray. That he hadn't wanted to tell me because he didn't want me to worry. That he was still flying home from work anyway—because of course he was; my dad is the most stubborn person I have ever met in my life—and that he was already mid-trip, with one more flight to go.

I swear I felt something cold move through my chest. Not shock. Not panic. Something deeper—like my body remembering what it's like to lose a parent.

There's a very specific kind of fear that lives inside people who've already lost one. It doesn't disappear with time. It just gets quieter until something wakes it up. And hearing my brother say "70s" and "gray" and "one more flight" woke it up instantly.

I just kept hearing it all in my head. My dad. Alone. On a plane. Above the clouds. Out of reach. Out of control. And the part that gutted me? He didn't even tell me. Because he didn't want me to worry. He didn't want to be a burden. Just like I didn't want to be one when I was 15 and my mom died. *Funny how patterns echo across generations.*

My brother kept talking, giving me the details he had, trying to stay calm for both of us, but I could feel the weight of it landing in my body one sentence at a time. The reality that this might not be just a scare. That I might be hours away from losing my last parent. That there was nothing I could do to stop it.

When we hung up, I just sat there.

I didn't move. I didn't run for my coat. I didn't open my laptop looking for flights to fly back to Saskatchewan. I didn't explode into tears the second the call ended. I didn't collapse into that old, familiar spiral when fear takes the wheel and drives me straight into panic. I just sat there, breathing like my body was asking me to stay with myself.

And it wasn't because I wasn't scared. I was terrified. I could feel it curled up in my stomach, tightening my throat, burning behind my eyes. I could feel grief's shadow standing right behind me, waiting. I could feel the same questions I asked myself at 15 clawing their way up again: *What if I don't have a parent tomorrow? What if I have to survive this alone? What if this is the night everything changes . . . again?*

But here was the difference: for the first time in my life, the fear didn't own me.

I felt it fully, but I didn't disappear inside of it. And that shocked me more than the phone call.

Because old me would've unraveled. I would've spiraled into the deepest parts of my mind, imagining the worst-case scenario, imagining walking into another funeral home, imagining being parentless before I even hit 33, imagining Maddie and Rhett never really knowing their grandfather. I would've Googled oxygen levels and heart attacks and whether flying at that altitude could kill someone. I would've convinced myself there was no hope. I would've been pacing, shaking, hyperventilating, disappearing into panic like it was my second home.

But this time I didn't.

I cried, but it didn't consume me. I imagined the worst, but I didn't live in it. I felt the fear, but I didn't abandon myself to it.

It was the strangest, most grounding thing I've ever experienced. I let the tears fall, but I stayed in my body. I let my hands shake, but I didn't run from the moment. I let myself feel the heartbreak of *I can't lose my dad, too*, and I didn't drown in it. I let myself think, *I don't have my mom here. How would I survive losing the only parent I have left?*—and somehow I still stayed.

I didn't numb. I didn't avoid. I didn't fall apart.

I held myself. I held the fear. I held the uncertainty. I held the grief that hadn't even happened yet. I held the possibility that my life could look completely different by morning. And underneath all of it—all the fear, all the questions, all the trembling—was this quiet, steady truth pulsing through my body: *no matter what happens, you will be okay. You will survive this. You will know what to do. You are not that 15-year-old girl anymore. You are a woman who can hold herself now.*

I've never felt anything like it. It wasn't confidence. It wasn't bravery. It was truth. A truth I had earned. A truth I had built. A truth I had lived myself into over years of identity work, self-trust work, heartbreak, rebuilding, choosing myself, choosing honesty, choosing growth.

This was the moment when all of it came together, in real life, in real fear, in the moment when I used to completely lose myself.

And this time, I didn't lose myself. I anchored deeper into myself.

When my dad finally landed safely, hours later, when my brother sent me the text that he was okay and was taking him straight to the hospital to get checked over, when the panic lifted and the world started spinning again—the relief hit me, of course. But the relief wasn't the thing that stayed.

What stayed was the realization: I have become a woman who can hold more life than I ever believed possible.

Everything isn't perfect. Fear didn't disappear. I'm not untouched by what I've been through. But I trust myself now. I trust myself to stay, even in the moments that shake me.

That night was the moment my identity caught up with me. The moment I realized self-trust isn't built in pretty chapters—it's built in the ones that rip something open. The moment I realized becoming *her* isn't about being fearless—it's about letting fear exist without abandoning your power.

And that's exactly where this chapter begins: with the truth that your next level has nothing to do with having an easy life or perfect circumstances. It's about becoming the woman who can hold all of it—the joy, the fear, the unknown, the expansion—without running from herself.

Capacity Is a Skill (Not a Personality Trait)

The wildest part about that night wasn't the fear. It wasn't the possibility of losing my dad. It wasn't even the grief that cracked open old wounds I thought had scarred over.

The wildest part was what happened after—in the days and weeks that followed—when I started noticing all the subtle, almost invisible ways I'd become a different woman without even realizing it.

You don't become the woman who can hold more in one big moment. You become her in the way you respond to everything after. That night didn't just show me who I was in a crisis. It showed me who I had already become in the smallest, quietest corners of my life—the parts no one sees, the parts I didn't even give myself credit for.

What I realized was this: capacity isn't something you're born with. It's something you build.

It's not personality. It's not luck. It's not some inherited trait passed down through generations. It's a skill. A muscle. A choice you make over and over again until it becomes your default. And the woman you become in your hardest moment is simply the sum of all the tiny, unrefined reps you've been putting in without realizing it.

In the weeks after that night, I started catching myself doing things that old me would've never done, things that felt so natural I almost missed them.

I'd walk into situations with a steadiness that didn't come from pretending to be strong. It came from being strong. Not loud strong. Not performative strong. Quiet, grounded, *I know who I am now* strong.

I didn't over-explain myself when I said no. I didn't spiral when something didn't go as planned. I didn't talk myself out of decisions before I made them. I didn't shrink when someone didn't agree with me. I didn't replay every conversation wondering if I sounded stupid.

Without even trying, I had stopped living like a woman who needed permission to exist. I was acting like a woman who trusted herself to hold her life—all of it.

And the contrast between old me and new me? It was sharp.

Old me would overthink every choice, like there was always a right and wrong answer and I was one misstep away from ruining my life. New me just chose. Quickly. Cleanly. Without apology.

Old me would walk into a room and immediately scan it for who I needed to become to keep the peace. New me walks in as myself and lets the room adjust.

Old me needed reassurance before taking any step forward. New me moves without waiting to be congratulated for it.

Old me panicked at the idea of disappointing anyone. New me knows disappointment isn't fatal—abandoning myself is.

These weren't huge, identity-altering decisions. They were micro-moments, the kind that stack up quietly until one day they hit you all at once. Like catching myself responding calmly to something that would've shredded my nervous system years ago. Or realizing I didn't feel guilty for taking up space. Or noticing how differently I held boundaries now—not as a defense mechanism, but as a way of honoring my energy. Or the first time I caught myself saying, "No, that doesn't work for me," without apologizing five times and offering a PowerPoint presentation proving why I had the right to say it.

Capacity shows up in these tiny shifts.

The moment you stop bracing for the worst the second something good happens. The moment you stop shrinking when someone compliments you because you don't know how to receive it. The moment you stop treating ease like it's suspicious. The moment you stop sabotaging opportunities because you're scared you won't be able to maintain them. The moment you let yourself want more without acting like you're greedy for it.

These are the signs. The markers of a woman expanding her capacity. Same life. Different way of showing up. The more I paid attention, the clearer it became: that night didn't create my capacity. It revealed it.

It revealed that I could sit with fear without letting it take over. It revealed that I could hold uncertainty without scrambling for control. It revealed that I could feel grief without collapsing into old wounds. It revealed that I had built a nervous system that didn't mistake discomfort for danger. It revealed that I had become a woman who didn't run from her life—I ran toward it.

And once you see that in yourself, you can't unsee it.

Once you realize your identity has shifted from survival to self-leadership, you start moving differently in every corner of your life. You stop living on the edge of burnout because you're no longer trying to be everything to everyone. You stop negotiating with your own standards because you trust yourself to follow through. You stop outsourcing your steadiness to how the day goes because you know you can anchor yourself no matter what the day brings.

- Capacity changes how you handle stress. It still shows up, but you don't spiral the same way or turn it into a story about what's wrong with you. You stay with it, and it moves through faster.
- Capacity changes how you move in relationships. People don't suddenly get easier, but you stop bending yourself to keep everything comfortable. You hold your ground without over-explaining or pulling back.
- Capacity changes how you approach your goals. They don't feel effortless, but you stop quitting before you've given yourself a real chance. You follow through more often, even when it's inconvenient or uncomfortable.
- Capacity changes how you hold joy. It's not constant, but you let it exist when it's there. You don't shut it down or brace for it to disappear. You allow yourself to experience it.

That's the difference between the woman I used to be and the woman I am now. My life did not magically became calm. That fear didn't magically evaporate. The grief can still knock the wind out of me.

The difference is that I don't crumble when life shakes. I don't collapse when things feel heavy. I don't let old stories drag me backwards. I hold myself. I stay with myself. I move with myself, even when the moment is too big, too scary, too uncertain for the woman I used to be.

Capacity is what happens when identity work becomes embodied—when *her* stops being an idea you reach for and starts being the woman you naturally show up as. It's not performative. It's not forced. It's not the "perfect version" of you. It's the real version of you, grounded in the truth that you can hold your life even when it gets loud.

And that's what I want you to see: you don't build capacity in the calm. You build it in the moments where you realize, *Oh . . . this would've broken me before. And now I'm still standing.* That's the reveal. That's the proof. That's the quiet transformation you notice only when life hands you a moment big enough to show you what you're made of.

The woman who can hold more isn't fearless. She's anchored. She's self-led. She trusts herself enough to not abandon herself when the stakes are high. And that identity—that grounded, expansive, self-honoring identity—is the foundation of everything that comes next.

When You Don't Have the Capacity Yet

Most women think they are stuck because they are unmotivated or inconsistent or sabotaging themselves again, but that's almost never the truth. What's actually happening is quieter, deeper, and so much more human: their lives are trying to hand them more than they have ever held, and their nervous systems are still calibrated to the girls they used to be.

So the moment something good shows up—the opportunity, the love, the visibility, the version of their life they've been praying for—they don't rise to meet it. They flinch. They pull back. They squint at it like it's suspicious. They tell themselves they are not ready. They convince themselves it's safer to wait. They try to make the dream smaller so they don't have to feel the weight of what stepping into it might require.

They think this makes them flawed. They think this means they aren't capable or disciplined or "strong enough" to level up.

But that's not it at all. It makes them human.

It's not failure that scares you. It's what comes after the yes. We're afraid of being seen with the light fully on. We're afraid of holding something beautiful and not dropping it. We're afraid of letting life feel good and then losing it. We're afraid of becoming the woman who can carry more than the version of ourselves we've rehearsed for years.

So when life hands us more, we freeze. We want it, but we don't know how to hold it.

It shows up in ways we don't even notice at first. You finally get a compliment you've been craving—on your work, your energy, your gift—and instantly brush it off instead of letting it land. Someone offers you an opportunity, something aligned, something expansive, and you suddenly become the busiest woman on earth, creating logistics problems that don't exist. You start getting momentum in your growth and then, out of nowhere, you pick the biggest fight with yourself or someone else, just so the progress stops before things get too good.

You feel yourself rising into a new identity and then the moment someone from your old world sees you, you shrink back into the girl they remember. You're on the edge of a breakthrough, the kind that could change everything, and that's exactly when you start procrastinating harder than ever. You tell yourself you're tired, overwhelmed, need a break, need clarity—anything to avoid the truth that you're scared of stepping into something you can't yet imagine yourself holding.

And I need you to hear this: none of those things make you weak. They make you a woman whose capacity hasn't caught up with her desire yet.

Here's what I mean. Wanting a bigger life doesn't magically give you the capacity to live it. Having a vision for your next level doesn't mean you immediately know how to carry it. Wanting the relationship, the business, the energy, the freedom, the confidence—doesn't mean your body knows what it feels like to hold that much truth, that much joy, that much responsibility, that much visibility.

Wanting more is a decision. Holding more is a skill. And most women were never taught the skill.

By now, you can see the pattern. You learned how to adjust, to accommodate, to stay within what felt manageable, and for a long time, that worked. But that version of you was built to handle less. So of course when life tries to hand you something bigger, you don't know how to carry it. Of course it feels foreign. Of course you second-guess it. Of course the inside of your body panics even when your mind is screaming, *I want this!*

Your next level will always require more capacity before it gives you more confidence. That's the part women misread. They think they need more confidence to say yes. But really, they need more capacity to hold what they said yes to.

So they freeze. They shrink. They disconnect from themselves. They ghost their own progress. They numb out with tiny distractions—scrolling, snacking, zoning out, organizing a junk drawer like it's a spiritual calling—anything to not feel the discomfort of expansion.

But let me paint the truth that no one tells you: this is not self-sabotage. This is your identity protecting you from a life you don't yet believe you can handle. This is your system choosing the familiar over the fulfilling. This is the old version of you trying to keep you safe from the expansion she wasn't built for.

And that fear? It's not a sign you're not ready. It's a sign you're close.

Fear is what your body feels the moment before your capacity grows. Fear is the doorway into who you're becoming. Fear is the friction between the woman you've been and the woman you're becoming—and friction is how identities change.

Your capacity grows in the uncomfortable. In the uncertain. In the stretch. In the moments that ask you to stay with yourself when the old you would've vanished into panic or distraction or doubt. It grows every time you choose presence over avoidance. Every time you let yourself feel something without shrinking. Every time you hold the moment you're in without trying to numb it, rush it, or escape it.

That's capacity. That's what makes you the woman who can hold more.

And the truth is, you already know what it looks like when you don't have the capacity yet. You've lived it. You've felt it. You've repeated the patterns enough times to know exactly how it plays out.

But you're here now, in this chapter, because you're ready to stop confusing those patterns with who you are.

Those reactions don't define you. They reveal where you're growing next. They're not proof you can't handle more. They're proof you're on the edge of becoming the woman who can.

The woman you're becoming isn't someone new. She's the unedited version of you, the one who wasn't allowed to exist when you were busy surviving. She's already inside you. Capacity is just the process of opening the door wider and letting her through.

When Good Starts Feeling Scary

No one prepares you for what happens after life starts to work. After the storm finally passes, the healing starts to settle, and you wake up one morning realizing that things are good. The chaos has quieted. The goals you used to daydream about have become normal. You're not drowning anymore, and you can finally exhale.

And yet, instead of peace, something strange happens.

You start bracing for impact. You start scanning for what could go wrong. You start waiting for the other shoe to drop.

It's such a subtle thing that you almost don't notice it at first—the way your body tightens even in the middle of joy, the way you downplay good news so you don't "jinx it," the way you can't just let yourself be happy without wondering how long it will last. You tell yourself it's realism, maturity, responsibility.

But underneath all that logic is fear.

The kind that whispers, *Can I really trust this?*

Because the truth is, for most of us, safety has never been found in ease. Safety was surviving chaos. Safety was earning approval. Safety was being the one who could handle it all. And when the noise goes quiet, when the striving slows down, it doesn't feel peaceful—it feels foreign. Your nervous system doesn't recognize stillness as safety yet. It feels like the moment before something bad happens.

So you create little storms.

You pick apart the good. You second-guess the timing. You find flaws in what you prayed for. You shrink the celebration before anyone else can take it away.

And you call it humility or balance, but what you're really doing is protecting yourself from disappointment. It's a survival reflex dressed up as self-control.

This is what no one talks about in healing: the fear of joy. The fear of ease. The fear of being seen as someone who's doing well.

We spend so long fighting to get out of pain that we never learn how to live without it. We get addicted to fixing. We get comfortable in the climb. And when the work starts working, our brain panics because it doesn't know who we are without something to chase or repair.

That's why so many women sabotage their next level. Feeling safe in the good requires a new identity. You can't keep living like the woman who only knows herself through struggle and expect to feel at home in success. You have to relearn what safety feels like when nothing's falling apart.

It might look like getting the job or the relationship you once begged for and then immediately finding new reasons to doubt it. It might look like being in a healthy relationship but feeling restless because there's no drama to decode. It might look like hitting an income milestone and suddenly feeling pressure to prove it wasn't a fluke. It might look like finally feeling confident in your body—and then finding something new to critique.

It's not self-sabotage for the sake of chaos; it's your body trying to return to what it knows.

Peace isn't proof that something bad is coming. It's proof that you're finally safe enough to rest.

Your body might not believe that yet—but your higher self does. The version of you who's been doing this work didn't come this far just to keep re-creating struggle. She came here to learn how to let it be good.

Letting things be good takes practice. It means staying with it instead of pulling away the second it feels unfamiliar.

It's noticing when your brain starts scanning for danger and saying, *We're safe now*. It's noticing when you start to shrink and reminding yourself, *I'm allowed to expand even when it's quiet*. It's noticing when you want to pull back from joy and choosing to stay open anyway.

You have to teach your body that it's safe in softness. That being calm doesn't mean the other shoe is about to drop. That good things can last. That joy doesn't make you naive—it makes you alive.

You don't have to keep apologizing for your happiness or downplaying your wins to make other people comfortable. You've earned the right to feel safe in your own success.

Expansion can feel lonely at first. You've shifted how you show up, and not everything around you reflects that yet. You're not available for the same stress responses anymore. The old cycles don't feel like home, and the new ones haven't fully formed. It's the in-between that makes you want to run back to struggle because at least struggle feels familiar.

But if you can hold the discomfort of calm long enough, something beautiful happens: you start to realize that peace isn't boring. It's powerful.

You start to trust quiet rooms. You start to find thrill in stability. You start to understand that calm doesn't mean nothing's happening; it means everything is integrating. You start to see that your joy doesn't make you unrelatable; it makes you magnetic.

This is the part of growth no one warns you about: when things get better, your fear doesn't vanish; it just changes shape.

It goes from *What if I fail?* to *What if I can't sustain this?* From *What if they don't like me?* to *What if they finally see all of me?* From *What if it never happens?* to *What if I lose it once I have it?*

But the antidote is the same: trusting yourself.

The woman who knows she can hold herself through the good and the hard stops bracing for loss. She stops micromanaging outcomes. She stops diluting her joy to make it feel safer. She lets herself feel the fullness of her own success because she knows that even if things shift, she'll still be okay.

That's what emotional maturity really is: not controlling everything, but trusting yourself to handle whatever comes.

So if you've found yourself waiting for the catch, questioning your blessings, or feeling ungrateful for wanting more—please know this doesn't mean you're unhealed. It means you're expanding. Your system is just catching up to the new level of safety you've created. You're teaching yourself how to exist in abundance without apologizing for it.

> *Letting things be good is one of the hardest lessons of all. Because it means surrendering control. It means believing you don't have to keep earning what's already yours. It means releasing the narrative that safety exists only in struggle.*

But once you start practicing it—once you start breathing through the good instead of bracing for loss—you realize that this is what you were fighting for all along.

You didn't do all that work just to survive. You did it so you could feel safe in joy. You did it so you could laugh without scanning for danger. You did it so you could stop mistaking chaos for passion and peace for emptiness. You did it so you could finally live in the life you built, not just manage it.

So when good starts feeling scary, remember this: fear is a sign that you're expanding beyond what your old self thought was possible. Your nervous system just needs time to catch up to your new reality.

The life you prayed for is not a test—it's a mirror. It's showing you that you are finally safe to receive.

The more you let yourself receive, the more safety you create. The more safety you create, the more joy you can hold. And the more joy you hold, the less you'll need struggle to remind yourself that you're alive. Because you'll know—deep down, undeniably—that you were built for both. You were built to heal and to thrive. To hold the ache and the awe at the same time. To let it be good and trust that you can handle that, too.

How *Her* Holds More

You eventually reach a point where your own patterns stop feeling like flaws and start looking like clues. Not shame, not failure—just evidence of where your capacity was capped. And once you see that your reactions weren't personal, they were protective, everything shifts. You stop making yourself wrong and start making yourself ready.

That's what holding more looks like. It's not about being unbothered or perfectly regulated. It's not about glowing through chaos or pretending you're above the things that used to break you. It's about the way you return to yourself. The way you stay inside your body. The way you respond instead of react. The way you carry your life instead of collapsing under the weight of it.

Fear still shows up. She just doesn't leave herself in it. She knows it's part of growth. She expects it. She meets it with steadiness instead of shame. She doesn't spiral into *Why am I like this?* or *I thought I was further along*. She's not looking for perfection—she's looking for presence. She knows her power is in staying with herself long enough to choose the response that matches who she's becoming, not who she's been.

That's what emotional capacity looks like: staying present with your feelings instead of letting them run the show. When something scares her, she breathes. When something triggers her, she pauses. When something feels bigger than she expected, she holds herself through it instead of outsourcing her safety. She doesn't run from discomfort or try to make it disappear. She lets it move through her, knowing discomfort is not proof she's failing—it's proof she's expanding.

Energetic capacity shows up differently. It's the difference between *everything drains me* and *I decide what gets access to my energy*. She doesn't wake up and hand her bandwidth to the world like it's owed to them. She protects her time. She protects her mornings. She protects her peace like it's part of her job description. And it is.

She doesn't apologize for needing space. She doesn't feel guilty for having limits. She doesn't confuse relational obligations with emotional responsibility. She knows her life can't grow if her energy is always in survival mode. So she rests without shame. She says no without a speech. She honors her cycles instead of forcing herself into hustle versions of womanhood she's done performing.

She doesn't rely on chaos to prove she's doing enough. She gets honest about what her life needs to run well. She builds systems that support who she's becoming, not who she was. She makes adult decisions her younger self avoided. She creates breathing room. She removes unnecessary friction. She doesn't call herself lazy when she's overloaded—she builds a life that makes alignment easier. She knows that expanding her life doesn't mean doing more—it means doing differently.

She doesn't shrink for anyone. She doesn't dilute herself to be easier to love, easier to accept, easier to understand. She doesn't silence herself to keep the peace. She doesn't pretend she's fine when she's not. She doesn't abandon her own truth because someone else can't hold it.

She knows that anyone who requires her to be small in order to love her never truly loved her; they loved the version of her that never made them uncomfortable. She doesn't carry that anymore. She learned how to let people misunderstand her without collapsing. She learned how to let relationships evolve without clinging. She learned to stop negotiating her worth in rooms that were never built for her expansion.

She doesn't panic every time money moves. She doesn't spiral when things fluctuate. She doesn't make money morality. She doesn't think wanting more makes her greedy. She doesn't pretend she's okay with "just enough" when she knows she was built for more than survival.

She learned how to let money feel normal. She learned how to receive without questioning it. She learned how to want more without shame. She learned how to hold abundance without waiting for it to disappear. She expanded her capacity for overflow by expanding her capacity for self-trust.

And here's the thread that ties all of this together: she holds more because she doesn't outsource her identity anymore. She doesn't wait for proof. She doesn't wait for permission. She doesn't wait for someone to choose her first. She doesn't need everything to be stable before she expands. She knows she creates stability by how she shows up, not what happens around her.

This version of you isn't built on confidence alone. Confidence might get you moving, but capacity is what enables you to stay. It's what holds you steady when things feel unfamiliar, when pressure rises, when old patterns start pulling at you again.

The difference now is in how you respond. You don't leave the moment it gets uncomfortable. You don't talk yourself out of what you want just because it stretches you. You don't shrink when something feels bigger than what you're used to. You stay with yourself through it. That's what changes everything. Not the absence of fear or perfect conditions, but your ability to remain with yourself in the moments that used to take you out.

That's how you start holding more. Not all at once, but in real time, as your life asks it of you. And once you learn how to do that, you stop questioning whether you can handle what you want. You already know you can.

The First Time I Realized I Could Hold More Joy, Too

The journal didn't start as a plan. It didn't start as a next move for my brand or some carefully mapped-out strategy. It started the same way most of the real, soul-led things in my life have: quietly, in the middle of normal life.

I was in my room doing that end-of-day shuffle, putting laundry away, grabbing socks off the floor, just moving things around like moms do when the house finally goes silent. *Her Inner Glo* already existed at that point—just me, my laptop, and those late-night posts I hoped would land somewhere. And out of nowhere, this thought dropped in: I should make a journal.

Not a book. Not a course. Not some massive product. Just a journal. Something simple. Something real. Something women could hold. Something that asked the kinds of questions I wish someone had asked me years ago.

It felt like a full-circle moment. Because when I left the Yukon—when I left my old life behind—the very first thing I bought was a pink Walmart journal. Blank pages. Nothing fancy. And I wrote in it like my life depended on it . . . because in a way, it did. I wrote out who I wanted to become, what I wanted my future to feel like, and the kind of woman I hoped I could grow into.

So sitting there years later, with laundry in my hands, realizing I was now creating the kind of journal I once needed myself. It felt like something inside me clicked into place. Like I wasn't just becoming her—I was finally creating from her.

Old me would've talked herself out of that idea before it even finished forming. Old me would've said, *Who do you think you are? You didn't finish high school. You're not a writer. You don't create things—you buy them from people smarter than you.* Old me would've waited for someone else to validate the idea.

New me didn't ask for permission.

I didn't tell anyone I was making it. I didn't poll my friends. I didn't create a pros-and-cons list. I just sat down on the side of my bed, opened my laptop, and started. It felt small. Almost laughably small. But it also felt like something only I could do. Something that came from the part of me that was finally waking up.

And maybe that's why I kept it to myself—because it felt sacred. Not fragile. Not embarrassing. Sacred. There's a difference. For the first time in my life, I trusted myself with something that mattered. I didn't need an audience. I didn't need applause. I didn't need anyone to tell me it was a good idea. I just needed me.

So I made it. Quietly. Slowly. In between wiping counters and switching laundry and getting snacks and living an everyday mom life. There was no cute process. No aesthetic notebooks. Just me and a laptop and a growing feeling in my chest that maybe I wasn't who I used to be anymore.

When I uploaded it to Amazon, I didn't tell a soul. I clicked publish with my heart pounding and immediately shut my laptop because the old voice in my head whispered, *Delete it before anyone sees it.* But another voice—the newer, steadier, one I had worked damn hard to hear—whispered back, *Let it exist.*

So I did.

And that night, I posted it on Facebook. No grand marketing plan. Just a picture of me holding the journal and a caption from a woman who was tired of waiting for permission to believe in herself. And that was that. I didn't expect much from it. I didn't expect anyone to care. I didn't hold high expectations for it. The point wasn't to impress anyone. The point was to prove something to myself.

The next morning, my phone rang. It was a family member. Someone who had seen my post. Someone who wasn't the type to hand out compliments lightly. I answered, expecting a casual chat.

Instead, I heard, "I saw your journal. I'm proud of you. This is inspiring, Alicia."

And something in me froze in disbelief. I wasn't used to holding praise like that. I wasn't used to letting it land. I wasn't used to letting myself feel seen in that way.

Old me would've laughed it off. Deflected it. Downplayed it. Said something like, "Oh, it's nothing," or "It's just a little project," or "I don't know if it's any good." Old me would've crushed the compliment before it ever had a chance to bloom.

But this time, I didn't.

I let it land. I let myself feel the warmth of someone seeing me clearly. I let myself feel proud. I let myself feel like maybe—just maybe—I was building something real. Something that meant something. Something that wasn't just a cute idea in my head, but evidence of the woman I was becoming.

My throat tightened and my chest felt like it was stretching to make room for a version of me who had always been there, waiting to be acknowledged. I remember standing in my kitchen after the call, hands resting on the counter, staring at nothing and thinking: I did that. Me.

The girl who once thought she'd never amount to anything. The girl who once believed she had no gifts, no potential, no voice worth listening to. The girl who let other people tell her who she was.

That girl was gone. I wasn't running anymore. The thing about moments like this is that they don't look impressive from the outside. Nobody claps when a woman learns to receive a compliment. Nobody celebrates when she lets herself feel proud instead of ashamed. Nobody throws confetti when she stops saying, "It's nothing," and starts saying, "Thank you."

But these are the moments that change everything.

These are the moments when a woman becomes her. Not because of the achievement itself, but because of who she becomes in response to it.

That day, something shifted. Quietly, like most shifts do. The way I moved through the rest of that morning felt different. I wasn't floating on a high; I wasn't hyping myself up. I was grounded. Certain. Steady.

I made my coffee slower. I put my hair up without rushing. I caught my reflection in the mirror and didn't look away. I saw someone I hadn't fully met yet—someone who could hold joy without shrinking. Someone who didn't need to dim her light to keep other people comfortable. Someone who didn't panic when good things came her way. Someone who didn't need to prove or perform or explain why she deserved to feel proud. Someone who was allowed to feel it.

And that's when I realized something big: capacity isn't just about holding fear. It's not just about surviving the moments that punch you in the chest. It's not just about staying grounded when life shakes you.

Real capacity is being able to hold joy without sabotaging it. To hold success without minimizing it. To hold pride without flinching. To hold a compliment without running. To hold the truth that you're becoming someone extraordinary—even when no one else sees it yet.

These two moments—my dad and the journal—were completely different stories, but the same identity shift. One showed me I could hold the hard. The other showed me I could hold the good.

And that's what this chapter is really about. Not strength in crisis. Not perfection in healing. Not confidence as an aesthetic.

It's about becoming the woman who can hold all of it—the fear, the joy, the uncertainty, the recognition, the praise, the expansion—without abandoning herself.

Because she isn't just the woman who survives the hard moments. She's the woman who lets good things stay. She's the woman who trusts herself when life shakes and when life blossoms. She's the woman who doesn't collapse when something beautiful enters her world.

She's the woman who can hold more life than she ever thought possible.

And if you've made it this far, if you're reading these words, then so can you.

Key Points

If you're going to take anything with you from this chapter, let it be these points:

- Capacity changes how you handle stress—not because stress disappears, but because you stop making stress mean something about you.
- A grounded, expansive, self-honoring identity is the foundation of everything that comes next.
- Wanting more is a decision. Holding more is a skill. And most women were never taught the skill.
- The woman you're becoming isn't someone new. She's already inside you.
- Emotional maturity is not trying to control everything but instead trusting yourself to handle whatever comes.
- Energetic capacity shows up differently. It's the difference between *Everything drains me* and *I decide what gets access to my energy*.

Chapter 8

Bold Is Your Baseline

It was a simple, steady afternoon. I had wrapped up a bit of work earlier—nothing major, just the kind of focused hour that leaves you feeling quietly proud. I was putting a few things away, moving through the house at an easy pace, not rushing for once. I picked up my phone without thinking, just a quick check before moving on. And then I saw the subject line: *Book Proposal Opportunity*.

For a solid three seconds, I didn't even register it. My brain did that thing where it auto-filters anything that feels too big into the spam category. I assumed it was a scam, or some random pay-to-publish thing I'd delete without thinking twice. But I clicked it anyway. Then I saw it. Wiley. An actual global publisher. A real imprint. Not a random Gmail account. Not a "Hey girl, want to write an e-book?" offer. A legitimate, old-me-would-have-never-even-googled-them-because-she-didn't-believe-she-belonged-there publisher . . . in my inbox. My stomach dropped and lit up at the same time.

I reread the first paragraph three times, waiting for the catch. Waiting for the "just kidding." Waiting for that one line that would prove this wasn't real. But it was. They had found my work. They had been watching. They were interested in my story, my voice, my message. They wanted to talk about a book. And that's when the tears came—not cute, glowy tears. The ugly, full-body, shoulders-shaking kind.

Because in that moment, every version of me tried to stand up at once. The girl who dropped out of high school. The woman who used to lie on job applications because she was terrified people would find out. The one who spent years convinced she wasn't smart enough, polished enough, or qualified enough to be anything more than background in her own life. They all rushed to the surface with the same question: How is this happening to us?

I could feel the familiar script starting to spool up in my head. You're not educated enough for this. You're not professional enough for this. You're going to embarrass yourself. Any minute now, they're going to realize they emailed the wrong girl. That voice had been with me for so long it practically had its own room in my mind. For years, it ran the show. It was the reason I stayed small, played safe, waited for permission. It was the reason I used to look at women with book deals and think, *Good for her . . . but that will never be me.*

But layered over top of that old soundtrack was something else. A voice that was calmer. Steadier. A voice I had been deliberately building, brick by brick, choice by choice. *Her.* The identity I'd been practicing long before I had any big, shiny evidence to point to. The woman I'd been writing as every night on Instagram when nobody was clapping yet. The woman who packed up her life in the Yukon that night and completely changed her life. The woman who had created a journal on a whim. The woman who had kept showing up even when posts flopped, launches fizzled, and algorithms did their thing.

And she wasn't shocked at all. *Of course, this is happening,* she whispered. *You've been living as me for a long time. This is just the world catching up.*

The contrast between those two voices was wild. One part of me was spiraling: *You? A book? With them? Are you insane?* The other part of me just felt . . . right. Like the universe had finally put on paper what I had already decided in my body. It was the first time in my life that something this big didn't feel like a fluke. It felt inevitable.

It wasn't luck or some special connection. By the time that email landed, I was already different. I had already been choosing bold in the dark. I had already been speaking like a woman who had something to say, not a girl hoping someone would let her sit at the table. I had already been moving like a woman who knew she was building something real. The email was proof, not permission.

That night, after the chaos of bedtime—pajamas half on, one sock in the hallway, kids calling "Mom!" for water they did not need—the house finally got quiet again. I sat at the kitchen table with my laptop open, the glow of that email staring back at me in the dark. I didn't open champagne. I didn't light a candle and set up some aesthetic "I got a book deal" moment. Being married to a blue-collar man means you don't always get to share things in real time. So, I took a screenshot and sent it. No context. Just the image and a "Look."

He called me immediately, still in his work clothes, camp noise buzzing in the background. I could hear the grin in his voice before he even said anything. "Babe. Holy shit." Hearing him say it out loud made it real in a way my brain was still catching up to. Tears started again, dripping onto the kitchen table while we laughed and swore and sat in that moment together, miles apart.

It wasn't captivating. It wasn't staged. No one was filming it for TikTok. It was just me in my messy kitchen, my husband in a camp room, two kids asleep down the hall, and this wild, quiet knowing settling over me: I didn't become her because of this email. I got this email because I already was her.

For so long, boldness had felt like a costume—something I had to psych myself up to wear. The first time I raised my prices. The first time I posted something online that felt "too much." The first time I said no without launching into a five-paragraph apology. I'd practically be shaking every time. Heart pounding. Fingers hovering over the button. Playing out every worst-case scenario in my head: *they'll judge me, they'll leave, they'll talk about me.* Boldness back then felt like putting on a jacket that didn't quite fit yet. I'd zip it up, breathe shallow, and think, *Who do I think I am?*

But sitting there with that email open, something clicked. This didn't feel like a moment where I was trying bold on. It felt like a moment that showed me bold was already in my bones. Because that email wasn't the first bold move I'd made—it was the result of hundreds of them. Every time I hit post when my voice was shaking, every time I told the truth instead of performing, every time I chose the uncomfortable aligned thing over the comfortable familiar thing, I was stacking proof. Not for a publisher. For me.

I had been building a life that matched *her* for years. That was the real work. The book deal was just one of the ways life mirrored it back. And that's what I want you to feel as you read this. We love to talk about big breaks like they're lightning strikes. One day she was nobody, the next day she had the deal, the platform, the life. But it doesn't work like that. The world doesn't hand bold opportunities to women who are still auditioning for their own lives. It responds to the women who already decided who they are.

By the time something big lands, the identity has usually been there for a while. That's what this moment taught me. Bold wasn't something I dragged out just for launches, brave conversations, or scary emails. Bold had quietly become my baseline. I had stopped treating it like a costume I brought out for special occasions and started wearing it like my own skin.

And maybe you know exactly what that inner tug feels like. That sense that you've been slowly becoming a different woman in the background, even if nothing on paper looks that different yet. The way you're less available for certain conversations. The way you don't swallow your opinions quite as often. The way you've started moving differently in rooms you used to shrink in. The way you catch yourself saying something honest and think, *Wow . . . old me would've never.*

This is that moment, zoomed in. An inbox. An email. My kids' toys still on the floor. My husband on FaceTime. And me realizing: bold doesn't feel like a show anymore. It feels like me.

This is about that exact pivot point when bold stops being a thing you hype yourself into and starts being the way you simply exist. The rest of this chapter is going to break that down: how you become the standard in your own life, what it looks like when bold is your baseline, and how that energy inevitably becomes magnetic. But it all starts here, in a moment like this one. A regular afternoon. A messy kitchen. An email you once would've thought was meant for someone "better." And the quiet, undeniable truth rising up inside you: of course, this is happening. Because you're not putting bold on anymore. You're living it.

When Bold Starts Rewriting the Room

The funny thing about that email is that it didn't just change what I believed was possible for me. It changed what everyone else thought they could expect from me, too. I was no longer available to show up as the watered-down version of myself they were used to. That's the part no one talks about when they say, "Be bold." They make it sound like a personality trait—be louder, be braver, be more "out there." But bold isn't a volume. It's a standard. It's the quiet, nonnegotiable decision that you're no longer going to treat your life like an accidental side-effect of other people's expectations.

Once that email landed, yes, there was excitement and pride and all the things. But there was also this very real, very grounding question: If I'm the woman a global publisher wants to build a book with, why am I still saying yes to things that don't even feel like my life? That's when I started noticing it—in the rooms I sat in, the conversations I tolerated, the things I let slide "because it's easier," the roles I played to keep the peace. Boldness didn't just show up in the big moves. It started rewriting the tiny ones.

It looked like this: the next time someone messaged me asking if I could "quickly" look over something that would actually take an hour, I didn't wrap my no in 15 apologies and a three-paragraph explanation about my schedule. I just said, "I don't have capacity for that right now." Full stop. The next time a friend made a sideways comment about "that Instagram thing," I didn't laugh it off and pretend it didn't sting. I didn't go into a long TED Talk trying to prove why what I do matters. I just looked at them, smiled, and said, "It's my work. And I'm really proud of it." Then I let the silence sit. The next time I was invited into something that sounded good on paper but felt off in my body—a collaboration, a group chat, a "we should totally do something together"—I didn't say yes because I was flattered. I let it be a no, even if it made me feel like I was "too much" or "ungrateful."

No one was handing me a microphone in any of those moments saying, "Look at this bold woman, everyone!" It was just me, in my everyday life, refusing to abandon the version of me that email reflected back. That's the sneaky thing about proof: once it arrives, you can't pretend you don't know who you are anymore. Bold, for me, stopped being about doing outrageous things and started being about not abandoning myself in ordinary ones. It was the way I responded to texts. The way I talked about my work. The way I stopped rushing to fill every silence with over-explaining. The way I let people adjust to the new standard instead of shrinking back to the old one. And slowly, the rooms started to adjust.

People stopped assuming I'd always be the one to bend. They stopped expecting me to say yes just because "you're so good at this" or "you're home anyway." They stopped treating my work like a hobby I'd drop the second someone needed something. I stopped participating in the version of myself that made that disrespect possible. That's what I want you to see about boldness: it's not just about the risks you take. It's about the tolerance you lower.

Bold is the woman who no longer laughs at jokes that hurt her and then overthinks it for three days after. Bold is the mom who stops saying "it's fine" when it's clearly not. Bold is the friend who doesn't sit through conversations that feel like character assassinations disguised as girl talk. Bold is the woman who stops begging people to see her value and starts living like it's nonnegotiable. And here's where it gets really powerful: the world starts to mirror back whatever energy you're the least willing to drop. When you're willing to drop yourself, everyone else gets used to that. When you're willing to drop your standards, everyone else leans on that. When you're willing to drop your truth to keep the vibe light, everyone else expects that.

But when bold becomes your baseline, something shifts. You stop being the flexible one who will "figure it out" no matter what. You stop being the emotional sponge for everyone's chaos. You stop being the woman people call when they want to vent but never change. You stop being the "low-maintenance" one at the expense of your own needs. Instead, you become the woman people think twice before unloading on, because they know you're not going to just nod along—you're going to lovingly ask, "So what are you going to do about it?" You become the woman whose no means no the first time, not after three tries. You become the woman whose yes means something, because it's not handed out like a participation ribbon—it's intentional, clean, and chosen.

Do people always like it? No. Some pull back. Some get defensive. Some say you've "changed." But you didn't become a harsher version of yourself—you became an honest one. Boldness, at its core, is just honesty with legs. It's the moment you stop lying about how okay you are. The moment you stop pretending you're not exhausted. The moment you admit, "I want more than this," and don't stuff it back down. The moment you say, "This isn't working for me anymore," and let the chips fall where they may.

The more you live from that place, the more obvious it becomes—to you and to everyone watching—that this isn't a phase. It's a new baseline. I think that's what that email really pulled into focus for me. It wasn't the achievement itself. It was the question it dropped into my everyday life: If I'm the woman who can hold something like this, what am I no longer available to pretend about? That's what I want to hand you here. Not a list of "bold things to do," but a question that will quietly change everything if you let it: If you fully believed you were already the woman your future life is built on, what would you stop pretending is okay?

The friendship that runs on your emotional labor? The relationship in which your needs are always second? The workplace that treats your brilliance like it's optional? The way you talk about yourself in front of your kids? Bold doesn't always look like leaving, quitting, or burning it all down. Sometimes it looks like staying—and showing up differently. Sometimes it looks like having the hard conversation you've been avoiding. Sometimes it looks like finally saying, "This is what I want," out loud. And just like that email did for me, those moments won't turn you into someone new. They'll reveal who you've been building all along.

That's the real magic: when life suddenly hands you proof, you're steady enough to match it. You're no longer trying to convince anyone you belong. You're busy living like you do. And that's when everything else in your world—conversations, relationships, opportunities—either rises to meet you or quietly falls away. Because you finally decided: this is who I am now.

When Your Old Self Stops Answering the Door

It shows up in small, unexpected moments. You reach for a reaction you've had for years, and it's just not there. The insecurity, the spiral, the familiar panic you used to fall into so easily. You expect it to show up, and it doesn't. And for a second, it almost throws you off, because you realize something in you has actually changed. I noticed this after the book deal email, but it wasn't because of the email itself. It was because when the old doubts tried to flare up—the ones that used to knock me flat—nothing inside me caught fire. I could feel the ghost of the old trigger, the shadow of the old fear, but my nervous system didn't grip it the same way. It was like my mind went, *Should we freak out?* and my body just shrugged. There was no panic. No spiral. No shame storm. Just a quiet, grounded sense of *Oh. We don't do that anymore.*

If you've ever tried to spiral and found that you couldn't access the same entry point, you know exactly what I mean. You go looking for the worry, expecting it to swallow you like it always has—and it doesn't show up. You start rehearsing the "what if everything goes wrong" monologue, and the words feel almost foreign in your mouth. You attempt to guilt-trip yourself into shrinking, and there's no emotional reaction to latch onto. It feels disorienting at first, like losing your footing in the best possible way. Because once you've expanded past certain versions of yourself, you can't squeeze back into them. Your body won't let you. Your mind can't pretend it believes those old stories anymore. Your nervous system refuses to collapse on command. You've outgrown the need to fold.

No one really prepares you for this part: the internal recoil. Your old patterns stop being believable. You can't force yourself to care about things you used to obsess over. You can't make yourself fear things you've already walked through. You can't pretend you're still the girl who would crumble under pressure when you've lived through enough to know better. It's the moment your system says, *We're done with that version. Try something else.* And if you're anything like me, your first reaction is confusion. You expect the old you to burst through the door the second something big happens—the insecure one, the doubting one, the one who spirals at the slightest hint of the unknown. You brace for her. You prepare for her. You even try to summon her, because she's familiar. But she doesn't come. She doesn't answer. She's not available anymore.

That's what this work does—not just the journaling, reflection, and rituals, but the way you've been choosing yourself in all the tiny, unfiltered moments. It doesn't make your life perfect. It doesn't remove fear from your world. It simply changes who has the microphone in your mind.

The woman you've been building in the background—the one you've been practicing being before you had evidence—she's the one who responds first now. She's the one steering the internal dialogue. She's the one setting the tone. And she's so woven into your system that the old reactions don't stand a chance.

The wildest part is how physical it feels. You go to drop into an old pattern—overthinking, catastrophizing, self-sabotaging—and there's a pause. A literal pause where your system checks in and goes, *Is this really what we're doing?* That pause is everything. That pause is proof. It's the upgrade you earned with every uncomfortable choice, every boundary you held, every time you showed up scared but still showed up. It's the return on all those moments you thought didn't matter.

And here's what makes this so magnetic: when your internal baseline shifts, your external world shifts with it. You move through the world differently when you're no longer fighting yourself. You don't question your worth the same way. You don't negotiate with your intuition. You don't hand your power to people who haven't earned it. You don't shrink to avoid being misunderstood. You don't panic at the unknown. You start living from a place that feels clean—not performative confidence, but grounded certainty. People feel it. Energy like that is unmistakable.

This is why new opportunities start showing up. You have stopped leaking your energy into old versions of yourself. When you stop spiraling on autopilot, you have space to notice what's available to you. When you stop rehearsing your fears, you free up mental bandwidth to create, to receive, to be seen. When you stop dragging your old self into every new moment, you finally meet the version of you who can walk through big doors without flinching.

And I don't want you to read this and think, *Wow, I can't wait until that happens to me.* I want you to realize it's *already happening.* If you're here, reading this, doing this work, there are moments in your life right now when the old reaction doesn't land the same way. Maybe tiny moments. Maybe ones you brushed off as nothing. But they're there: the pause before you spiral. The breath you take before apologizing for something that wasn't your fault. The way you hold your own gaze in the mirror a second longer than you used to.

These are not coincidences. They're cracks in the old armor—the light coming through. Proof that the woman you're becoming isn't theoretical. She's already inside you, shaping how you move even when you don't notice it. If you want to lock that in even deeper, here's a simple question to keep in your back pocket for the moments when the old version tries to pull you back: *Is this actually me . . . or is this who I used to be?* Just naming the difference changes the way the moment feels. Awareness breaks the spell. Your choices do the rest.

This is the point in your journey when you stop trying to act like her and start realizing you already are her. Where your old self stops answering the door. Where the spirals don't hit the same. Where the fears don't stick like they used to. Where you catch yourself standing taller, breathing slower, thinking clearer, trusting deeper—with no performance, no push, no trying. Just being. That's what becomes possible when bold becomes the baseline you lead from without even thinking. And that internal shift? It quietly sets the stage for every single external shift that comes next.

The Words That Set Me Free

Long before there was a journal, a book deal, a community, or anything that remotely resembled a brand, there was a much quieter moment. No publisher. No audience. Just me, a couch, a baby monitor, and a restless tug in my chest I couldn't ignore anymore.

It started quietly, like most of the biggest shifts do. There wasn't a plan. No strategy. No "I'm going to start a movement" moment.

By then, I'd been in therapy for a while. I was learning to tell the truth to myself. I was learning to breathe again. But every night, after the house went quiet and the noise of the day faded, I'd feel it—the ache that said, you're meant for more than just surviving.

I didn't know what "more" meant. I just knew it wasn't another "goals" list or another affirmation on my mirror. I wanted connection. Real, messy, human connection. I wanted to know if anyone else felt like they were healing and holding it together with duct tape at the same time.

So one night, I opened my laptop. It was late—that strange, sacred hour when courage sneaks in because exhaustion has softened all your defenses. My cursor blinked on a blank Facebook status box, and I just started typing. I didn't think about what I was supposed to say. I just said what was true. I wrote about how hard it was to feel grateful and heavy at the same time. How becoming a mom cracked me open in ways therapy couldn't. How healing didn't feel graceful—it felt like losing versions of myself I'd been taught to hold onto. I wrote about how no one talks about the in-between—the part where you're doing the work, but you still feel like you're made of glass.

I stared at the words, my heart pounding. It felt too raw. Too revealing. I hovered over post for what felt like forever, hearing every old narrative screaming at me: *You're not qualified to talk about this. You'll sound dramatic. People will think you're unstable.* And then another voice whispered back, quieter but steady: *Or maybe . . . they'll see themselves in it.*

So I hit post. Then I slammed my laptop shut and immediately regretted it. I sat there in the dark, stomach twisted in knots, mentally preparing myself to delete it. But before I could, my phone buzzed. Then again. And again.

The comments started coming in. Messages from women I hadn't spoken to in years. A coworker. A high-school friend. A cousin I haven't seen. "Wow, this is exactly how I've been feeling. I thought I was the only one who struggled with this. Thank you for saying it out loud."

And in that moment, something clicked. The ache that had followed me for years—the one that whispered no one understands—loosened its grip. I realized I wasn't alone. None of us were. We were all just too scared to go first. That night changed everything.

I didn't suddenly have a business. I didn't suddenly have a brand. I just had proof that honesty lands. Every time I shared a piece of my story after that, I felt lighter. Hiding was exhausting. Every time I told the truth, I reclaimed a piece of my energy that shame had been hoarding.

I started small—stories about healing, motherhood, losing my mom, finding myself again. I never wrote from the pedestal of *I've figured it out*. I wrote from the trenches. I wrote from the middle. And to my surprise, that's what people connected to most. One night, a woman messaged me and said, "You put words to something I didn't know how to say." I remember staring at that message and crying. Because for so long, I didn't have words either. And now, somehow, my words were helping someone else find hers.

That's when I realized that telling my story wasn't self-indulgent—it was self-return. There's a lie women are fed that says, "You can't lead until you're healed. You can't speak until you're certain. You can't share until it's tidy." But the truth? Our real power lives in the middle of the mess.

When I started writing publicly, I was still healing my relationship with myself. I was still doubting my worth. I was still scared of being judged. But I showed up anyway—shaky hands, unfinished thoughts, all of it. And what happened next wasn't just growth. It was liberation.

Women started DMing me late at night like I was their diary. They told me about the marriages they were questioning, the dreams they'd buried, the versions of themselves they missed. And it hit me: this is what I'd been craving—truth that doesn't need a filter. The more I shared, the more I saw how starved women were for someone to say, "Me, too." Not in a hashtag way. In a human way.

And that's what *Her Inner Glo* became—not a brand, not a coaching business: a home for our humanity. Every post I wrote was a declaration that healing wasn't about perfection; it was about permission. Permission to be seen while you're still figuring it out. Permission to speak before your voice stops shaking. Permission to let your truth breathe, even if it makes people uncomfortable.

And, yes, it did make people uncomfortable. Not everyone got it. Some unfollowed. Some whispered. Some said I was "oversharing." But the women who stayed—they were my proof that vulnerability doesn't scare the right people away; it draws them closer. Because when one woman uses her voice, it gives a hundred others permission to use theirs.

That's the part that still gives me chills—the thought that one late-night post written by a scared woman on her couch could ripple into thousands of women choosing themselves, their healing, their truth. It taught me that your story is never just yours. It's the bridge between who you were and who you're becoming—and the invitation for others to cross, too.

Looking back, I can see that sharing my story was its own kind of therapy. Every caption, every message, every me too stitched something back together in me. It helped me grieve my mom in a new way—because now, instead of wishing she could see the woman I've become, I could be the kind of woman she would've wanted me to be: one who speaks truth even when it shakes.

The more I wrote, the less I performed healing and the more I embodied it. I wasn't chasing a perfect life anymore. I was creating an honest one. And that's what I want every woman to understand: your voice matters because it's real, not because it's polished. Your truth doesn't have to sound profound to be powerful. It just has to be yours.

Because the moment you start telling the truth about your life, the shame loses its power. The moment you stop trying to make your pain pretty, it becomes purpose. And the moment you decide that your voice belongs in the room, you stop waiting for someone else to hand you permission.

That's what changed everything for me. That one decision: to speak. And I think that's what women everywhere are craving—not more advice, not more steps, not more how-tos. They want proof that they're not the only ones figuring it out as they go. They want to see a woman who's not afraid to say, *I'm healing, and I'm still here.*

Because when you share from a real place, you remind every woman reading that she can, too. And maybe that's what healing actually looks like. The courage to turn pain into purpose. The willingness to use the past to heal. The decision to speak while your voice still trembles.

That's what *Her Inner Glo* was built on. Truth. Truth spoken by a woman who finally decided that her story mattered, even while it was still being written. And maybe that's what you're here to remember, too. That your story doesn't have to be wrapped in a bow to be worth telling. That your voice is medicine—not once you're healed, but because you're healing. And that when you go first, you give the women watching permission to stop hiding, to stop waiting, and to start living their own truth out loud.

Somewhere, there's a woman scrolling in the dark, just like I was—heart racing, tears in her eyes—waiting for someone to remind her that her story still matters. Maybe tonight that someone is you.

The Proof of Magnetism

Let's talk about when reality finally catches up to the energy you've been building in the dark. A moment that doesn't feel like luck or timing or coincidence—it feels like recognition. Alignment. Evidence. The instant the world stops asking who you think you are and starts responding to who you already decided to be.

For me, that moment looked like a number on my phone. Two years after I started *Her Inner Glo*. The day it happened was just an ordinary day. I opened my phone, refreshed my profile, and there it was: 100,000.

A hundred thousand women choosing to be in my world. A hundred thousand women resonating with a voice I once believed didn't matter. A hundred thousand women saying, "Me, too . . ." to the fear, the doubt, the desire, the truth. "Me, too . . ." to the parts of themselves they had edited down to survive.

For a quick moment I stared at the number like it had to be a glitch. And yet—there it was. Proof that this work doesn't just shift the way you feel. It shifts the frequency you live at. And that frequency calls people in.

But the number wasn't the part that rewired me. What came after did.

We were in Saskatchewan visiting my dad, my brother, and my precious new nephew, Gabe. I walked into my dad's house after running an errand with my brother and sister-in-law, and there they were: giant rose gold balloons spelling out 100K. My kids were bouncing around, shrieking with excitement they didn't fully understand. My husband was grinning, proud in a way that made my throat tighten instantly. He's always been like that—the man who tells strangers about my Instagram like it's a world tour announcement, the one who never lets me downplay the movement I'm building. The one who cheered for my arrival long before I did.

And then my dad looked at me and said, "So, 100K, hey?" He paused for half a second—just long enough for my heart to catch—and then he said the one line he's repeated my whole life after every win, big or small: "Dad got proud of you."

People outside my family would hear it and think nothing of it. But to me, it was everything—recognition layered with years of history, love, humor, and meaning. And the second he said it, something inside me cracked open in a way I wasn't prepared for.

A few years earlier, I would've deflected it. Laughed it off. Swallowed the compliment before it had a chance to land. I didn't know how to hold pride back then. I didn't know how to receive anything that reflected a version of myself I didn't yet believe I was.

But standing there in that doorway, balloons floating behind me, my babies tugging on my legs, my husband grinning, my dad smiling, I didn't shrink. I didn't flinch. I didn't perform humility as a shield. I let it in. Fully. Cleanly. Completely. The woman I had become knows she is allowed to be proud. She knows that receiving recognition is not arrogance. It's alignment.

I leaned against the wall, trying to steady myself as the weight of what was happening finally landed. This moment had nothing to do with social media. Nothing to do with numbers. Nothing to do with vanity or metrics or validation. It was proof. Proof that the girl who thought she had nothing to offer had become a woman whose words touched lives she'd never meet. Proof that when a woman stops waiting for permission and starts owning her truth, her life shifts in ways logic can't explain. Proof that boldness is contagious—and the world responds to the energy you choose to live in.

I thought about the younger version of me—the one who spent years convinced she'd never be enough. The one who used to dream about becoming her but always followed it with, *But not me*. I thought about how many nights I had almost given up, how many times I had posted something and instantly regretted it, convinced I'd gone too far, too loud, too bold. And then I looked at those balloons and realized, *I am her*. Not because of the milestone—but because of every micro-moment that led here. Every shaky post. Every honest caption. Every boundary I finally held. Every moment I chose truth over performance. Every time I refused to shrink.

That's what 100K represented—not fame, not success, not achievement. Proof of magnetism. Proof of embodiment. Proof that bold had become my baseline. This isn't about turning into a bold woman. It's about realizing you already are one—and the world is simply catching up.

What made this moment so magnetic wasn't the number. It was the fact that my kids were watching. They didn't understand the milestone. They didn't understand the significance. They just saw their mom being celebrated. They saw me receiving pride instead of rejecting it. They saw me standing tall in my own life without apologizing for the space I take up. And I knew in my bones that this was shaping them in ways I'll never fully see—modeling courage, modeling confidence, modeling a woman who didn't wait to be chosen before she chose herself.

When you live boldly, you don't just change your own life. You change what your kids believe is normal. You change the energy of your home. You change the standard of what's possible for the women watching you. Boldness isn't personal—it's generational.

And that's why this moment was never really about me. It was a reminder—loud and undeniable—of what happens when a woman stops negotiating with her potential. It was the physical representation of boldness compounded. When you stop auditioning. When you stop waiting. When you stop performing smallness. When you stop pretending you're not meant for more. When you start living as her, even before the world understands it. That's when everything shifts.

The balloons eventually deflated. The number kept climbing. The moment passed. But the identity didn't. What stayed with me was the truth that rewrote everything: I didn't get 100K and become her. I became her—and 100K arrived.

And if boldness can take a girl like me—a girl who once felt invisible, unworthy, unqualified—and turn her into a woman standing in her dad's living room with evidence of her impact floating above her in rose gold balloons, then boldness can do the same for you. Because this was never about a milestone. It was about energy. Embodiment. Proof.

The thing no one tells you about becoming this woman is that there's always a moment right after the proof lands where you're forced to decide who you are now. Not in theory. Not in journaling prompts. In real time. When the evidence is sitting right in front of you and your only job is to rise to match it. That moment is quiet. It doesn't arrive with fireworks or dramatic music. It arrives exactly like this—in a doorway with balloons, in a kitchen with an email open, in an ordinary second that suddenly reveals how far you've come. Proof doesn't change you. It just shows you who you've already become. What you do with that truth is the real shift.

That's why boldness matters. It makes you steady enough to receive the things you once thought were impossible. Every bold choice you've made so far—every honest moment, every boundary, every yes that matched your future instead of your fear—has been training your nervous system for this exact season of your life. The season when the outside world starts to mirror back the woman you've already been living as in private.

And now, here's the part that matters most: once you reach this point, once bold stops feeling like a performance and starts feeling like your baseline, there's only one question left: What are you going to do with it? Not in some far-off future. Not once you "feel ready." Now. Because this is the turning point in every woman's rise: the moment where she stops waiting for more signs and starts choosing to live as the evidence herself.

Key Points

Take a moment with this. These are the pieces to carry forward:

- Boldness is not just about the risks you take. It's about the tolerance you lower.
- A bold woman stops begging people to see her value and starts living like it's nonnegotiable.
- Boldness, at its core, is just honesty with legs. It's the moment you stop lying about how okay you are.
- This work doesn't make your life perfect. It doesn't remove fear from your world. It simply changes who has the microphone in your mind.

Chapter 9

You Were Never a Project

Do you ever get tired of treating yourself like a renovation? Tired of waking up every morning scanning for flaws, calculating how much more "fixed" you need to be before you're allowed to feel proud of who you are? Tired of living like you're always one step behind the version of yourself you think you're supposed to become? That moment—the one where you stop dragging yourself through self-improvement like it's a punishment—is where everything changes. Because here's the truth no one told you growing up: you were never a problem to solve.

You were never meant to live inside a constant evaluation. You were never meant to measure yourself against milestones, expectations, versions of yourself that only counted if they were polished. You were never meant to wake up every day already losing. And yet, so many women do exactly that without even realizing they're doing it. Maybe that's been you. Maybe you've spent years treating your life like a checklist: be better, be calmer, be prettier, be smarter, be less emotional, be more productive, be everything except the actual human you are. Maybe you've spent years believing you'll finally be "enough" once you reach some imaginary version of yourself—the one who never doubts, never spirals, never slips, never breaks, never fears.

But that version isn't *her*. She's not perfect. She's not polished. She's not a statue carved out of confidence. She is the woman who decides the war with herself is over. She's not flawless. She just doesn't abandon herself anymore. When you stop treating yourself like a project, something wild happens: the noise quiets. The part of you that's always been scanning for what's wrong starts to loosen its grip. You no longer need to obsess over whether you're becoming *her* fast enough, because you finally understand the truth the world never taught you: you already are her in every moment you choose to stay on your own side.

This shift isn't subtle. You notice it right away. It's the moment you stop negotiating with your worth. It's the moment you stop auditioning for your own approval. It's the moment you stop tearing yourself down every time you show a crack. And it's the moment your whole life expands.

> *The woman who is done treating herself like a problem is the woman who becomes powerful without even trying.*

She's not performing anymore. She doesn't need to convince herself she's enough—she knows "enoughness" isn't something she earns; it's something she protects.

You've worked hard on yourself. It's brought you back to who you are beneath the self-doubt, the shame, and the stories you've been carrying for years. This chapter—this final moment between us—is about honoring that. It's about helping you see what's been true the entire time: you were never meant to fight yourself to become her. You were meant to come home to her. And the way you come home is by becoming the safest person you know.

Not the most disciplined. Not the most confident. Not the most healed. The safest. The woman who doesn't abandon herself at the first sign of doubt. The woman who doesn't tear herself apart when she's overwhelmed or insecure. The woman who doesn't punish herself for slipping into old habits or taking longer than she hoped. The woman who, when things get messy, doesn't turn inward with blame; she turns inward with warmth.

That's safety. And safety is the birthplace of self-worth. When you are safe with yourself, you no longer need external proof to feel like enough. You no longer need someone else to validate you before you choose yourself. You no longer need every moment to go perfectly in order to trust your own resilience. You stop spinning stories about your value based on your productivity, your body, your bad days, your mistakes, your slow seasons. Safety means you can tell the whole truth about your humanity without flinching.

You can say, "I'm scared," "I'm healing," "I'm frustrated," "I'm growing," "I'm learning," "I'm proud of myself," "I'm not abandoning myself today," and every version of you—past, present, and future—exhales in relief. When you become the safest place you know, you stop performing. You stop proving. You stop living like you're two steps behind a woman you were always meant to be standing beside. You start moving through your life with a softness that doesn't dilute your strength—it deepens it.

This is where she lives. Not in perfection. Not in achievement. Not in evidence. In how you treat yourself when no one is watching. This is the part of the journey so few women talk about: the emotional shift where you stop using self-improvement as a weapon and start using self-compassion as a foundation. Where you stop trying to "fix" your way into self-worth and start realizing you were worthy before any fixing was ever done. Where you stop being at war with your own reflection and finally let yourself see the woman who has survived, risen, healed, and grown in ways most people will never fully understand.

And here's the part that might surprise you: when you *stop* trying to fix yourself, you grow faster. Then, you're no longer burning energy fighting your own becoming. You're no longer afraid of falling behind. You're no longer tightening around every mistake. You're no longer teaching your nervous system that every dip means failure. You finally have space to breathe. And women who can breathe can rise.

The truth is, you've carried so much responsibility. You've navigated heartbreak, relationships, friendships, money stress, identity shifts, trauma, doubt, pressure, expectations—and for many of you, motherhood—while still showing up for your life.

And yet, you've been so conditioned to look for where you fall short that you forget how extraordinary you already are. This chapter—this moment—is your reminder that you don't need to become anything other than the woman you already are when you stop fighting yourself.

She's been here the whole time. Waiting. Watching. Whispering. Ready. The woman you're becoming isn't a distant dream. She's not a final version of you at the end of some perfect path. She's the you who emerges the second you stop abandoning yourself. She's the you who steps forward when you soften. She's the you who rises when you stay on your own side.

You don't need more proof. You don't need more confidence. You don't need more time. You just need to stop treating yourself like a problem. Because when you do? Everything changes. Your choices shift. Your presence sharpens. Your relationships deepen. Your life expands. Your joy stops being conditional. Your self-worth stops being a debate.

And you finally understand the truth this entire book has been building toward: you were never becoming her. You were remembering her.

What You've Been Searching For Was Never Confidence—It Was Permission

Every woman thinks she's chasing confidence. She thinks if she could just wake up one morning and finally feel fearless, finally feel worthy, finally feel certain, then she'd become the version of herself she's been dreaming about. So she chases it. She reads the books. She listens to the podcasts. She makes the vision boards. She writes the affirmations. She tries to talk herself into believing she is enough. And yet, even after all the work, all the effort, all the hoping, she still doesn't feel it. She still wakes up with that familiar ache—that quiet question in her chest asking, *Why don't I feel different yet?*

You're not lacking confidence. You're lacking permission. Confidence is a result. Permission is the beginning. Permission is the key that unlocks everything you've ever wanted from confidence: the peace, the power, the self-trust, the belonging. But permission isn't something the world teaches us to give ourselves. We're taught to wait for approval. To wait for readiness. To wait for a sign. To wait for someone else to validate our desires before we claim them out loud. We're trained to hold our breath until the world tells us it's our turn.

And so we become women who live in hesitation. Women who look at their lives and whisper, "Who am I to want this?" Women who dim their own dreams because they're waiting for someone—a partner, a parent, a boss, a friend, a stranger on the internet—to tap them on the shoulder and say, "You're allowed. Go." But the woman you're becoming? The woman whose identity you've been building piece by piece through this entire book? She stopped waiting a long time ago. Permission is the moment she pulls the power back into her own hands. It's the moment she stops asking the world for a stamp of approval and starts approving herself. It's the moment she realizes that nothing she wants—not the life, not the dream, not the soft mornings, not the big moves—requires anyone else's authorization.

And once a woman tastes that truth, her entire life changes. When you stop waiting for someone else to validate your desires, the shame around wanting more disappears. You stop apologizing for your needs. You stop shrinking your dreams to make them easier for other people to digest. You stop watering yourself down so you don't take up too much emotional space. You stop stretching yourself thin to keep the peace. You stop negotiating with your own worthiness like you're always one mistake away from losing it. Permission turns the volume down on every voice in your head that was never yours to carry. The ones that told you to be humble. To be grateful for what you have. To not ask for too much. To not make anyone uncomfortable with your ambition or your softness or your power. Permission lets you finally hear your voice again, the one that's been whispering under the noise for years.

When you start listening to that voice, you begin choosing differently. You feel more allowed to want the life that lights you up. Allowed to take up space without apology. Allowed to stop performing for approval you don't even need. Allowed to live in a way that feels like you. This is the identity shift most women spend their whole lives circling without ever naming it. It's about reclaiming authority over your own becoming. It's about realizing that you are the only one who gets to decide who you are, what you want, how you move, what you tolerate, and who you choose to be from this moment forward.

Permission is the moment you stop living from your past and start living from your potential. It's the moment you stop editing yourself into a version of smallness and start expanding into the fullness of who you already are. It's the moment you stop fighting your own desires as if they're dangerous. Your desires are not the threat—your hesitation is. Imagine your life if you stopped asking, *Am I allowed?* And started asking, *What would my life look like if I trusted myself completely?* Imagine if you didn't wait until you felt perfect to start the thing. Imagine if you didn't wait until you felt worthy to choose the boundary. Imagine if you didn't wait until you had evidence to back yourself. Imagine if you stopped holding your breath and finally let yourself exhale.

The moment you grant yourself permission, confidence becomes a side effect. When you choose yourself without apology, confidence shows up. When you trust your voice even while it shakes, confidence grows. When you take action before you feel ready, confidence builds. When you stop abandoning yourself, confidence becomes your baseline. But it all begins with permission. And you don't have to earn it. You don't have to prove anything for it. You don't need to cross a finish line for it. You can give it to yourself right now, in this moment, without fixing a single thing about who you are.

So ask yourself—gently, honestly, without overthinking: Where have you been waiting for permission that only you can give? Where have you been dimming yourself because you're scared of being misunderstood? Where have you been trying to earn the right to want what you want? Where have you been telling yourself *one day*, when what you really mean is *when I'm finally allowed to feel worthy*? Because the truth you've been circling since page one is this: you were allowed the whole time.

Her—the identity you've been stepping into—isn't the woman who waits. She's the woman who decides. She's the woman who moves. She's the woman who claims herself without hesitation. She's the woman who understands that self-worth isn't something she earns through perfection—it's something she protects by staying loyal to herself. And the moment you choose that? The moment you stop asking, *Am I allowed to be her?* . . .you become her.

The Moment You Realize You Finally Belong to Your Own Life

Sometimes it just clicks. You see yourself differently, and it stays. And from that point on, things don't feel the same. For me, that moment arrived on a morning that looked like my life—not polished, not curated, not picture-perfect, just real. The kids were wrapped up in their own little world, my husband was home on holidays, coffee was cooling on the counter, and out of nowhere this calm washed over me. A kind of calm I had never known in my earlier years, because I had never felt safe enough, grounded enough, or present enough to experience it.

I wasn't thinking about goals or metrics or the next thing I needed to fix about myself. I wasn't measuring, comparing, or chasing anything. I was simply standing in the middle of my own life . . . and I liked who I was in it. I finally felt like someone I wanted to come home to.

That realization hit deeper than any milestone ever could. Because for so many years, I didn't know what it felt like to belong to myself. I belonged to my fears, my insecurities, my doubts, other people's opinions, other people's expectations. I lived in a body I didn't trust, with a mind that rehearsed old stories on loop, and with a heart that was bracing for disappointment even on the good days.

But standing there in that room—nothing fancy, nothing staged—I felt something click into place. A kind of recognition. A remembering. A settling. As if every version of me that had fought to get here finally exhaled at the same time.

It wasn't pride in a loud sense. It was pride in a truthful sense. It was the realization that I had built a life I felt safe in, and I was the reason it felt that way. My internal world had changed. The way I spoke to myself had changed. The way I treated myself had changed. The way I stayed with myself—in discomfort, in joy, in the ordinary—had changed. And suddenly, I could feel the difference. Suddenly I knew right there and then that no matter what life threw at me, I could back myself. I got me.

Because the girl I used to be . . . she wouldn't have recognized this moment. She wouldn't have recognized me. She would've stood in the same kitchen and looked for what was missing. She would've critiqued the state of the house, worried about being too emotional, felt guilty for resting, or wondered whether she deserved to feel this peaceful. She would've looked at a beautiful life and convinced herself she was somehow failing at it.

But the woman I've become—through years of unlearning, through choosing myself when it felt unnatural, through tiny, unpoetic acts of belief—she stood there that morning and felt ownership. She felt rooted. She felt like someone worthy of the life she was living.

That was the real transformation. Not the business. Not the milestones. Not the achievements. It was the moment I could look at my life and see that I was no longer performing in it. I was living in it. Fully. Softly. Unapologetically. As me.

And I want you to hear this: you do not need a replicated moment like mine to experience that shift. Your version of this will be your own. It might happen while you're brushing your teeth. Or while you're driving home. Or while you're sitting on the edge of your bed in last night's oversized T-shirt. It might happen in a moment that looks painfully ordinary—until suddenly it isn't.

Because the real magic isn't the scene. It's the recognition. It's the moment you realize you no longer feel like a visitor in your own life. It's the moment you stop trying to impress a version of yourself that never existed in the first place. It's the moment you stop trying to earn worthiness and finally feel it in your bones. It's the moment you understand that the love, pride, softness, joy, and belonging you've been chasing were never meant to be external proof. They were meant to be internal truths.

When I stood there feeling something I'd never felt before—not fear, not self-consciousness, not the urge to escape or improve or shrink—I understood something that changed me forever: This wasn't a finish line. It wasn't "arrival." It was homecoming. The kind of homecoming that isn't about walls or routines or family dynamics but about finally living inside a version of yourself that feels true. A version of yourself you don't apologize for. A version of yourself you don't walk away from. A version of yourself that doesn't need to be fixed before she deserves peace.

And this is where your story folds into mine. Because this chapter is not just about what I realized. It's about what becomes possible for you when you stop looking for evidence that you're enough and start acting like a woman who already is. Your moment will be different. Your reasons will be different. Your life will be different. But the feeling—the soft, grounded, soul-deep knowing that you belong to yourself? That part is universal.

And once you feel it—once you truly feel it—everything else in your life shifts around it. Your boundaries change. Your standards rise. Your relationships evolve. Your self-talk transforms. Your dreams expand. Your energy recalibrates. Because you finally stopped abandoning yourself long enough for the truth to surface.

Everything you've been searching for was already yours. You just hadn't been standing in it.

The Legacy You Carry, Even When You Don't See It

The work stops being about fixing what hurt you. It becomes about recognizing what has always been true about you. It's the moment you stop obsessing over who you still need to become and start recognizing who you already are. It's the morning you wake up, catch your reflection in the bathroom mirror, and instead of bracing or critiquing yourself, you soften. You look at the woman staring back and feel something unfamiliar and holy: recognition. Affection. Home. That is where your legacy begins.

You've spent years being taught to measure yourself by achievement, approval, and performance. You learned how to shape-shift. How to self-monitor. How to preshrink. How to show only the safest pieces of yourself. And because of that, you became someone who could build a life but never fully inhabit it. Someone who knew how to keep up appearances but not how to belong to herself. This chapter is where all of that ends. When you realize that worthiness was never something you had to earn. It was the ground beneath your feet the entire time.

Your real legacy has nothing to do with what you achieve. It isn't the house, the job title, the milestones, the followers, or the applause. Those things fade. Your real legacy is in the way you treat yourself in the quiet, unfiltered moments no one sees. It's in the tone you use when you talk to yourself on the days you're struggling. It's in the gentleness you offer your own doubt. It's in the way you choose not to abandon yourself, even when it would be easier to. This is the kind of legacy that changes generations. Not just through children you may or may not have, but through every woman who crosses your path. Every friend who watches you rise. Every colleague who sees you stop apologizing for existing. Every stranger who catches a glimpse of your energy and thinks, without knowing why, *I want to live like that, too.*

Because this work was never just about raising daughters who feel worthy. It's about raising a world that feels safer because *you* finally do. Even if you never have kids, you are mothering something: truth, permission, possibility, a new kind of womanhood. When you start treating your desires like they matter, you teach every woman around you that desire isn't frivolous, it's direction.

When you begin honoring your needs instead of abandoning them, you shift the standard for every relationship you touch. When you soften toward your own reflection, you make space for other women to soften toward theirs.

This is how identity work becomes legacy work. When you decide you're already enough—before the transformation, before the milestones, before the evidence—your entire presence changes. You move differently. You speak differently. You walk into rooms with an energy that says, *I'm not here to prove anything. I'm here because I belong.* And that energy gives other women permission to question everything they've been taught about worthiness, too. It makes them wonder what life would feel like if they stopped negotiating with their own value. It makes them ask, *What if I'm already enough, too?*

There is something powerful about a woman who finally believes she is worthy. She admits when she's tired and rests without guilt. She lets herself want things she used to talk herself out of. She stops depending on the world to confirm who she is. And when she does, the world responds because she stopped abandoning herself long enough for people to feel her presence.

That's what self-love is. It's the relationship you have with yourself. It's the way you hold yourself after you fail. It's the tenderness you extend to the scared parts of you. It's the decision to stop talking to yourself the way people who hurt you once did. It's choosing to treat your own heart with the same softness you've given everyone else for years. It's standing in the belief that you're allowed to take up space, as you are.

And when you hold yourself like that, something shifts in every part of your life. You stop shrinking in relationships because you're no longer asking to be chosen. You stop performing for approval because you finally approve of yourself. You stop tolerating what drains you because you realize your peace is not optional. You stop over-explaining. You stop apologizing for existing. You stop asking for permission to be who you are. And the women around you—friends, coworkers, strangers on the sidelines of your life—they feel it. Your rise becomes an invitation. Your presence becomes a permission slip.

This is how your life creates a ripple effect. It's built in how you show up, not how perfect you are. Through a woman who finally decides her life is worthy of her own respect. When you walk into rooms with that kind of grounded energy, other women straighten their backs without knowing why. When you laugh without self-monitoring, they loosen their own edges. When you make choices from alignment instead of fear, they start to question where they've been settling. Your existence becomes an example because you stopped dimming yourself long enough for your life to be seen.

And the most important part? None of this requires you to become a different woman. It requires you to stop abandoning the one you already are. Underneath the conditioning, the fear, the old narratives, the pressure, the self-doubt—you've always been enough. You've always been powerful. You've always been capable. You've always been her. You just couldn't hear your own truth over the noise of everything you'd been taught to fear.

This is the mic drop of the entire book:

You don't have to become her. *You're already* her.

The work isn't about transforming yourself into someone new—it's about clearing the noise that made you forget your own magic. It's about understanding that your worthiness is not a performance, but a birthright. It's about realizing that the dreams inside you aren't random—they're direction. They're invitations into the life meant for you.

You are already leaving a mark. You are already rewriting the story. You are already building an inner world that reflects the woman you've been trying to become. You are already doing the work most women never give themselves enough credit for: you are showing up for yourself. Again and again. Even when it's messy. Even when it's slow. Even when you doubt. You are rising.

And that? That is legacy.

You're Already Her

There is no version of you that you need to chase. No shinier, more perfect, more healed, more impressive self waiting out on the horizon. No future milestone where you'll suddenly "deserve" the life you want. The woman you keep imagining isn't a future identity you have to earn—you are the truest, most unfiltered version of who you already are. All that's left is remembering her.

Somewhere along the way, you learned to believe that you needed to be more before you could feel enough. Somewhere, someone convinced you that worthiness had prerequisites—achievements, confidence, discipline, beauty, proof. You learned to delay your own life until you met a standard you didn't even create. You learned to wait for permission to feel proud of yourself, to trust yourself, to soften into the life that wants you. You learned to believe that joy and ease and belonging were rewards for women who had earned them, not women who were simply human.

But here's what no one told you: being her isn't about faking anything. It isn't about pretending to be confident or putting on a performance of strength. It isn't about manifesting some future version of yourself into existence. Being *her* is about removing everything that has been layered on top of you—all the doubt, all the conditioning, all the guilt, all the pressure—until what's left is the woman you were before the world told you who to be.

And that's why this part of the journey feels so different. Because for the first time, you're not striving. You're not hustling for worthiness. You're not dragging yourself through self-improvement to feel like a woman who matters. This isn't a glow-up rooted in insecurity. This is a reclamation, a remembering. A soft, grounded exhale that says, *I don't need anything outside of me to validate who I am.*

You are already her when you wake up in the morning before you've done a single productive thing. You are already her when you open your messy notes app and pour out something honest. You are already her when you sit in your car feeling overwhelmed and choose not to abandon yourself this time. You are already her when you show compassion to the parts of you that used to make you feel ashamed. You are already her when you speak gently to yourself instead of harshly. You are already her when you give yourself permission to rest. You are already her when you allow yourself to want more without apologizing for it.

Your worth has never been waiting for a milestone. It has never been tied to your body, your income, your title, your relationships, your productivity, your car, your house or your past. Your worth was woven into you the moment you arrived on this earth—untouched, unchanged, unmoved by anything that has happened since. Life may have convinced you otherwise, but deep down, a part of you has always known there was more to you than the fear you carried.

You don't have to fix yourself to live a life that feels good inside. You don't have to become the perfect version of yourself before you allow softness, connection, joy, love, belonging, or rest. You do not need to earn peace. You do not need to "deserve" a new beginning. You do not need to look different, achieve more, or impress anyone to feel like a woman worthy of her own life. You get to feel proud now. You get to feel capable now. You get to feel chosen by yourself now.

Being her *is not a destination; it is a decision.*

A daily one. A quiet one. A sometimes shaky one. But a decision nonetheless—a decision to stop abandoning yourself. To stop assuming something is wrong with you. To stop negotiating with your worth. To stop waiting until you have more evidence. To stop believing the lie that you must arrive somewhere before you are allowed to feel like enough.

You are enough because you are here. Period.

And when you really let that truth in—not just intellectually, but in your body, in your breath, in the way you move through your day—everything begins to shift. Your standards rise naturally. Your boundaries stop feeling like walls and start feeling like self-respect. Your relationships begin to reflect the way you treat yourself. Your dreams stop feeling far away and start feeling like extensions of who you already are. You stop seeking permission and start recognizing your own power. You stop waiting to be chosen and start choosing yourself.

It's about closing the gap between who you think you need to be and who you already are. It's about letting yourself be seen by yourself. It's about waking up one morning, catching your reflection, and realizing you finally look like a woman you trust.

When you start living from this grounded place—the place where you know you're enough without needing to prove it—your entire life begins to reorganize on that truth because clarity creates alignment. When you're not wasting energy performing, perfecting, or pretending, you have space to live. You have space to feel. You have space to pursue what you want. You have space to breathe.

You stop asking, *How do I become her?* and start asking, *What parts of me have I been ignoring that were her all along?*

You are not late to your life. You are not behind. You are not missing anything. You are not too much, too emotional, too sensitive, too messy, too soft, too loud, too quiet, too anything. You are a human being who has survived more than anyone will ever fully know—and you're still here, still rising, still choosing, still trying. That alone makes you extraordinary.

And the world tries so hard to convince women that they need to be different before they can feel enough. But you? You're done with that game. You're done with shrinking to fit. You're done with waiting for permission. You're done with performing worthiness. You're done with the exhausting pursuit of perfection. You're done with believing your power lives somewhere outside of you.

Because the truth—the real truth—is that the woman you want to become is not waiting for you in the future. She is sitting inside you right now, asking you to stop running from her. Asking you to stop dimming her. Asking you to stop postponing the life she knows you deserve. Asking you to trust that everything you've been searching for has been inside you this entire time.

She is not an aspiration. She is an unveiling.

And every time you choose honesty over fear, softness over self-criticism, presence over performance, alignment over approval—you meet her more fully. You embody her more deeply. You remember her more clearly.

You're already her.

Not someday. Not once you "fix" yourself. Not after the next milestone. Now—in this moment—simply because you exist.

And when you start living from that, your life finally meets you there.

One Last Thing

If I could sit across from you right now—not as the author of this book, not as the woman on Instagram, not as the version of me you've come to know through these pages—but as a human being who genuinely wants to see you rise, there's something I would want to tell you before you close this book and step back into your life.

I would want you to know that nothing in you is accidental. Not the way your heart works. Not the fire you keep trying to smother because you're scared it'll burn too bright. Not the softness you've been taught to treat like a weakness. Not the dreams that won't leave you alone, no matter how many times you've talked yourself out of them. Not the way you love, the way you hope, the way you feel things deeply. None of it is a flaw. None of it is extra. None of it is too much. All of it is intentional.

I would want you to know that your life will not change because you become a different person—it will change because you finally stop abandoning the person you already are. Nothing in this world is more powerful than a woman who stops asking to be chosen and chooses herself instead. A woman who stops negotiating with her own desires. A woman who stops apologizing for wanting more out of the life she's living. A woman who decides to trust herself, even on the days she feels shaky.

And yes—there will be days you forget everything you've read in this book. Days when doubt feels louder than truth. Days when old patterns try to drag you back into versions of yourself you've already outgrown. Days when you will look in the mirror and not immediately see the woman you've become. That does not mean you've failed. That does not mean you're back at the beginning. That does not mean you lost the progress you worked so hard for. It means you're human—and you're learning to stay with yourself through all of it.

If I could tell you one thing that would change your life, it would be this: *stay*. Stay with yourself when it feels uncomfortable. Stay with yourself when you don't have the answer yet. Stay with yourself when your mind is loud and your heart is tired. Stay with yourself instead of running back to the familiar. Stay with yourself instead of performing for belonging. Stay with yourself long enough to hear the truth beneath your fear. Because the woman you are becoming is built through presence.

I would want you to know that every dream you carry is asking something simple of you: let yourself want it. Not only if it fits everyone else's comfort level. Let yourself want what you want. Let yourself imagine a life that stretches you. Let yourself follow the pull you keep trying to logic your way out of. Let yourself be seen in the fullness of who you are, even if you shake the first time you do it.

And I would want you to remember that none of this is supposed to be effortless. Growth isn't clean. Becoming isn't linear. Confidence isn't constant. You are not here to nail it on the first try. You are not here to avoid discomfort. You are not here to live a small, quiet version of yourself just because it's easier. You are here to build a life that feels like it belongs to you. You are here to carry your truth in a way you never have before. You are here to show the next woman what's possible just by existing fully.

Your life is already a ripple, whether you realize it or not. Someone is watching you in the quiet way small moments leave a mark. The way your friend sees you hold a boundary and suddenly feels brave enough to hold her own. The way a stranger notices you softening toward yourself and wonders if she's allowed to do the same. The way a coworker hears you speak honestly and feels a spark of something she forgot she had. The way a child, yours or someone else's, witnesses the way you treat yourself and learns how to treat themselves, too.

Your becoming is never just yours. It radiates. It spills. It touches people in ways you may never know. And that is not a burden—it is an inheritance. One you give simply by choosing to live awake.

You are not nearly as far from the woman you want to be as you think. She is not waiting on a future version of your life. She is not holding out for the perfect moment. She is not hiding behind some milestone you haven't hit yet. She is here. In your voice. In your breath. In the way your body softens when you stop fighting yourself. In the way your intuition tugs at you. In the way your heart aches for more. In the way you're still reading these words because something in you knows you're meant for a life that feels good to wake up to.

You don't need to earn her. You don't need to deserve her. You don't need to chase her. You just need to stop walking away from her.

And if I could say one final thing—the thing I want echoing in the back of your mind when you wake up tomorrow—it would be this: you don't have to wait to live a life that feels like yours. Not later. Not once everything lines up. Right now. In the middle of your becoming. In the middle of your mess. In the middle of your brilliance. In the middle of your beautifully imperfect, deeply human life.

Choose yourself in the smallest moments. Back yourself in the uncertain ones. Trust yourself in the quiet ones. Love yourself in the messy ones. Show up as the woman you want to be, even if your hands shake a little. And remember, truly remember—that nothing about you is missing.

You're already *her*. And the world is better for it.

Key Points

Before you move on from these pages, let this stay with you:

- The moment you grant yourself permission, confidence becomes a side effect.
- Anything becomes possible when you stop looking for evidence that you're enough and start acting like a woman who already is.
- Self-love is believing you deserve to take up space—not because you proved it, but because you're human.
- You don't have to fix yourself to live a life that feels good inside. You don't have to become the perfect version of yourself before you allow softness, connection, joy, love, belonging, or rest.
- Remember that you're already *her* and the world is better for it.

Part Three

CLOSER AND REFLECTION

Part Three Closer: Living It, Owning It, Expanding It

If you've made it here, you're not the same woman who opened this book. Maybe the outside of your life hasn't exploded with change yet—or maybe it has—but internally, you've shifted. Quietly. Deeply. Permanently. The kind of shift that doesn't need a spotlight to be real. Women don't rise in obvious ways. They rise in the micro-moments, in the pauses, in the softness, in the decisions no one sees, in the standards they refuse to lower, in the way they return to themselves over and over again.

Part Three isn't about becoming someone new. It's about recognizing the woman you've worked this whole time to meet—and finally letting her lead. You've shed identities that never belonged to you. You've reclaimed parts of yourself you thought were gone. You've learned to hold more life—the good, the hard, all of it—without abandoning yourself. You've built a foundation of self-trust that doesn't shake the minute life gets loud.

This is what arrival feels like. Not a finish line—a beginning. A life built from alignment, not fear. A voice that no longer whispers. A woman who can hold more than she ever believed possible. Fear is still there. She just stays with herself through all of it. The next chapter of your life won't be written by the girl you were. It will be written by the woman who knows who she is now. And she's ready. Not someday. Now.

Close this section knowing one thing with absolute clarity: you are not waiting for your magic. You're living in it.

Part Three Reflection: Live from Who You Are Now

Before you step out of this book and back into your life, pause. There's been a shift in you, and you can feel it. You've walked through truth. You've walked through becoming. And now you've walked into the part of yourself that was waiting for you all along.

This isn't the chapter of your life where you try to hold onto the work. This is the chapter where you realize the work is already living in you.

You're not the woman who began these pages. She brought you here, but she's not the one leaving. The woman closing this book breathes differently. Decides differently. Sees herself differently. She knows too much about her own strength, her own truth, her own capacity to ever return to the version of herself who doubted whether she could handle her own life. You don't have to force that realization. Just notice it. Notice how your body feels steadier. Notice how your thoughts feel clearer. Notice how your truth feels louder. That's not inspiration. That's identity.

So as you stand here at the end of this part—and at the beginning of the rest of your life—ask yourself gently, honestly, boldly:

- What part of me is already living the life I used to only imagine?
- What truth about who I am now feels undeniable, even if no one else can see it yet?
- What becomes possible when I stop negotiating with the woman I've finally become?

These aren't questions to fix anything. They're invitations to witness yourself. To see the woman who's been slowly, quietly rising inside you with every honest moment, every aligned decision, every time you chose to stay with yourself instead of abandoning who you were becoming.

Now choose one action—one real, grounded, fully embodied action—that a woman like you takes. Not to prove anything. Not to earn anything. Simply because it matches who you are now. Maybe it's speaking a truth you've been holding back. Maybe it's raising a standard you've been lowering. Maybe it's letting yourself want more without shrinking. Maybe it's choosing the path you've known was yours long before you felt ready. Whatever it is, let it be a declaration, not a performance. A claiming, not a question.

Because that's what this book has been about. Not becoming *her*—but learning how to live from *her*. Owning it. Expanding it. Letting the woman you've been building take up space without waiting for permission or proof. And as you close this book—as you step back into your life—carry this with you:

I don't need to wait to be her. I can choose her now.

This isn't about having everything figured out. It isn't about getting it perfect. It's about how you decide to show up from here. You'll still have moments where you doubt yourself. Moments where you fall back into old patterns. That doesn't mean you've lost it. It means you're human. What matters is that you come back faster. That you choose yourself again.

That's where everything changes. Take what you've learned and bring it into your real life. Into your decisions. Into your voice. Into the way you move through your days.

Go live it. Own it. Expand it.

Not someday. Now.

This is where you stop waiting and start living like *her*.

Acknowledgments

To my kids: thank you for loving me through all of this, even when Mommy was writing instead of playing monster trucks or dress-up. I know your patience didn't always stretch that far. But hearing you say you're proud of me means everything.

To my husband: thank you for believing in me and reminding me who I am when I forget. You've been there through all of it, and I don't take that for granted.

To my dad and brother: thank you for loving me so loudly. For always reminding me how proud you are of me and never letting me forget it. That kind of love stays with me in everything I do.

To my husband's family, who became my own: thank you for loving me like your own and for being such a steady, supportive part of my life. Motherhood and this work wouldn't be possible without you.

To my friends: thank you for cheering me on, for seeing me, and for reminding me that the way I move through life matters. Your words have carried me more than you know.

I am so deeply grateful for all of you.

About the Author

Alicia Arlene is the founder of *Her Inner Glo* and a leading voice in identity-led self-leadership, known for challenging women to stop waiting and start living as the woman they already know they're meant to be.

Her work is rooted in lived experience. After losing her mom to cancer at 15, Alicia spent a decade in depression, low self-worth, and deep disconnection from herself. The woman people know now was not built from confidence. She was built from the moment Alicia decided she was no longer willing to keep living half-alive. What followed was years of choosing herself, rebuilding her identity, and creating a life that once felt completely out of reach.

Without a traditional educational path, Alicia built a thriving online platform and business, growing an audience of over 100,000 women, and securing a global book deal. Her work stands as proof that self-trust, self-leadership, and conviction create results.

Today, she is known for her direct, no-nonsense approach to personal growth, teaching women how to own their voice, back themselves fully, and build lives that truly feel like theirs.

Index

S